ANTISATIRE

The Other Voice in Early Modern Europe:
The Toronto Series, 70

Medieval and Renaissance
Texts and Studies

Volume 564

The Other Voice in Early Modern Europe: The Toronto Series

SERIES EDITORS Margaret L. King *and* Albert Rabil, Jr.
SERIES EDITOR, ENGLISH TEXTS Elizabeth H. Hageman

Previous Publications in the Series

MADRE MARÍA ROSA
Journey of Five Capuchin Nuns
Edited and translated by Sarah E. Owens
Volume 1, 2009.

GIOVAN BATTISTA ANDREINI
Love in the Mirror: A Bilingual Edition
Edited and translated by Jon R. Snyder
Volume 2, 2009

RAYMOND DE SABANAC AND SIMONE ZANACCHI
Two Women of the Great Schism: The Revelations *of Constance de Rabastens by Raymond de Sabanac and* Life of the Blessed Ursulina of Parma *by Simone Zanacchi*
Edited and translated by Renate Blumenfeld-Kosinski and Bruce L. Venarde
Volume 3, 2010

OLIVA SABUCO DE NANTES BARRERA
The True Medicine
Edited and translated by Gianna Pomata
Volume 4, 2010

LOUISE-GENEVIÈVE GILLOT DE SAINCTONGE
Dramatizing Dido, Circe, and Griselda
Edited and translated by Janet Levarie Smarr
Volume 5, 2010

PERNETTE DU GUILLET
Complete Poems: A Bilingual Edition
Edited by Karen Simroth James
Translated by Marta Rijn Finch
Volume 6, 2010

ANTONIA PULCI
Saints' Lives and Bible Stories for the Stage: A Bilingual Edition
Edited by Elissa B. Weaver
Translated by James Wyatt Cook
Volume 7, 2010

VALERIA MIANI
Celinda, A Tragedy: A Bilingual Edition
Edited by Valeria Finucci
Translated by Julia Kisacky
Annotated by Valeria Finucci and Julia Kisacky
Volume 8, 2010

Enchanted Eloquence: Fairy Tales by Seventeenth-Century French Women Writers
Edited and translated by Lewis C. Seifert and Domna C. Stanton
Volume 9, 2010

GOTTFRIED WILHELM LEIBNIZ, SOPHIE, ELECTRESS OF HANOVER AND QUEEN SOPHIE CHARLOTTE OF PRUSSIA
Leibniz and the Two Sophies: The Philosophical Correspondence
Edited and translated by Lloyd Strickland
Volume 10, 2011

The Other Voice in Early Modern Europe: The Toronto Series

SERIES EDITORS Margaret L. King *and* Albert Rabil, Jr.
SERIES EDITOR, ENGLISH TEXTS Elizabeth H. Hageman

Previous Publications in the Series

In Dialogue with the Other Voice in Sixteenth-Century Italy: Literary and Social Contexts for Women's Writing
Edited by Julie D. Campbell and Maria Galli Stampino
Volume 11, 2011

Sister Giustina Niccolini
The Chronicle of Le Murate
Edited and translated by Saundra Weddle
Volume 12, 2011

Liubov Krichevskaya
No Good without Reward: Selected Writings: A Bilingual Edition
Edited and translated by Brian James Baer
Volume 13, 2011

Elizabeth Cooke Hoby Russell
The Writings of an English Sappho
Edited by Patricia Phillippy
With translations by Jaime Goodrich
Volume 14, 2011

Lucrezia Marinella
Exhortations to Women and to Others If They Please
Edited and translated by Laura Benedetti
Volume 15, 2012

Margherita Datini
Letters to Francesco Datini
Translated by Carolyn James and Antonio Pagliaro
Volume 16, 2012

Delarivier Manley and Mary Pix
English Women Staging Islam, 1696–1707
Edited and introduced by Bernadette Andrea
Volume 17, 2012

Cecilia del Nacimiento
Journeys of a Mystic Soul in Poetry and Prose
Introduction and prose translations by Kevin Donnelly
Poetry translations by Sandra Sider
Volume 18, 2012

Lady Margaret Douglas and Others
The Devonshire Manuscript: A Women's Book of Courtly Poetry
Edited and introduced by Elizabeth Heale
Volume 19, 2012

Arcangela Tarabotti
Letters Familiar and Formal
Edited and translated by Meredith K. Ray and Lynn Lara Westwater
Volume 20, 2012

Pere Torrellas and Juan de Flores
Three Spanish Querelle *Texts:* Grisel and Mirabella, The Slander against Women, *and* The Defense of Ladies against Slanderers: *A Bilingual Edition and Study*
Edited and translated by Emily C. Francomano
Volume 21, 2013

The Other Voice in
Early Modern Europe:
The Toronto Series

SERIES EDITORS Margaret L. King *and* Albert Rabil, Jr.
SERIES EDITOR, ENGLISH TEXTS Elizabeth H. Hageman

Previous Publications in the Series

BARBARA TORELLI BENEDETTI
Partenia, a Pastoral Play: A Bilingual Edition
Edited and translated by Lisa Sampson and Barbara Burgess-Van Aken
Volume 22, 2013

FRANÇOIS ROUSSET, JEAN LIEBAULT, JACQUES GUILLEMEAU, JACQUES DUVAL AND LOUIS DE SERRES
Pregnancy and Birth in Early Modern France: Treatises by Caring Physicians and Surgeons (1581–1625)
Edited and translated by Valerie Worth-Stylianou
Volume 23, 2013

MARY ASTELL
The Christian Religion, as Professed by a Daughter of the Church of England
Edited by Jacqueline Broad
Volume 24, 2013

SOPHIA OF HANOVER
Memoirs (1630–1680)
Edited and translated by Sean Ward
Volume 25, 2013

KATHERINE AUSTEN
Book M: A London Widow's Life Writings
Edited by Pamela S. Hammons
Volume 26, 2013

ANNE KILLIGREW
"My Rare Wit Killing Sin": Poems of a Restoration Courtier
Edited by Margaret J. M. Ezell
Volume 27, 2013

TULLIA D'ARAGONA AND OTHERS
The Poems and Letters of Tullia d'Aragona and Others: A Bilingual Edition
Edited and translated by Julia L. Hairston
Volume 28, 2014

LUISA DE CARVAJAL Y MENDOZA
The Life and Writings of Luisa de Carvajal y Mendoza
Edited and translated by Anne J. Cruz
Volume 29, 2014

Russian Women Poets of the Eighteenth and Early Nineteenth Centuries: A Bilingual Edition
Edited and translated by Amanda Ewington
Volume 30, 2014

JACQUES DU BOSC
L'Honnête Femme: The Respectable Woman in Society *and the* New Collection of Letters and Responses by Contemporary Women
Edited and translated by Sharon Diane Nell and Aurora Wolfgang
Volume 31, 2014

LADY HESTER PULTER
Poems, Emblems, and *The Unfortunate Florinda*
Edited by Alice Eardley
Volume 32, 2014

The Other Voice in Early Modern Europe: The Toronto Series

Previous Publications in the Series

JEANNE FLORE
Tales and Trials of Love, Concerning Venus's Punishment of Those Who Scorn True Love and Denounce Cupid's Sovereignity: A Bilingual Edition and Study
Edited and translated by Kelly Digby Peebles
Poems translated by Marta Rijn Finch
Volume 33, 2014

VERONICA GAMBARA
Complete Poems: A Bilingual Edition
Critical introduction by Molly M. Martin
Edited and translated by Molly M. Martin and Paola Ugolini
Volume 34, 2014

CATHERINE DE MÉDICIS AND OTHERS
Portraits of the Queen Mother: Polemics, Panegyrics, Letters
Translation and study by Leah L. Chang and Katherine Kong
Volume 35, 2014

FRANÇOISE PASCAL, MARIE-CATHERINE DESJARDINS, ANTOINETTE DESHOULIÈRES, AND CATHERINE DURAND
Challenges to Traditional Authority: Plays by French Women Authors, 1650–1700
Edited and translated by Perry Gethner
Volume 36, 2015

FRANCISZKA URSZULA RADZIWIŁŁOWA
Selected Drama and Verse
Edited by Patrick John Corness and Barbara Judkowiak
Translated by Patrick John Corness
Translation Editor Aldona Zwierzyńska-Coldicott
Introduction by Barbara Judkowiak
Volume 37, 2015

DIODATA MALVASIA
Writings on the Sisters of San Luca and Their Miraculous Madonna
Edited and translated by Danielle Callegari and Shannon McHugh
Volume 38, 2015

MARGARET VAN NOORT
Spiritual Writings of Sister Margaret of the Mother of God (1635–1643)
Edited by Cordula van Wyhe
Translated by Susan M. Smith
Volume 39, 2015

GIOVAN FRANCESCO STRAPAROLA
The Pleasant Nights
Edited and translated by Suzanne Magnanini
Volume 40, 2015

ANGÉLIQUE DE SAINT-JEAN ARNAULD D'ANDILLY
Writings of Resistance
Edited and translated by John J. Conley, S.J.
Volume 41, 2015

The Other Voice in Early Modern Europe: The Toronto Series

SERIES EDITORS Margaret L. King *and* Albert Rabil, Jr.
SERIES EDITOR, ENGLISH TEXTS Elizabeth H. Hageman

Previous Publications in the Series

FRANCESCO BARBARO
The Wealth of Wives: A Fifteenth-Century Marriage Manual
Edited and translated by Margaret L. King
Volume 42, 2015

JEANNE D'ALBRET
Letters from the Queen of Navarre with an Ample Declaration
Edited and translated by Kathleen M. Llewellyn, Emily E. Thompson, and Colette H. Winn
Volume 43, 2016

BATHSUA MAKIN AND MARY MORE WITH A REPLY TO MORE BY ROBERT WHITEHALL
Educating English Daughters: Late Seventeenth-Century Debates
Edited by Frances Teague and Margaret J. M. Ezell
Associate Editor Jessica Walker
Volume 44, 2016

ANNA STANISŁAWSKA
Orphan Girl: A Transaction, or an Account of the Entire Life of an Orphan Girl by way of Plaintful Threnodies in the Year 1685: *The Aesop Episode*
Verse translation, introduction, and commentary by Barry Keane
Volume 45, 2016

ALESSANDRA MACINGHI STROZZI
Letters to Her Sons, 1447–1470
Edited and translated by Judith Bryce
Volume 46, 2016

MOTHER JUANA DE LA CRUZ
Mother Juana de la Cruz, 1481–1534: Visionary Sermons
Edited by Jessica A. Boon and Ronald E. Surtz. Introductory material and notes by Jessica A. Boon. Translated by Ronald E. Surtz and Nora Weinerth
Volume 47, 2016

CLAUDINE-ALEXANDRINE GUÉRIN DE TENCIN
Memoirs of the Count of Comminge *and* The Misfortunes of Love
Edited and translated by Jonathan Walsh
Volume 48, 2016

FELICIANA ENRÍQUEZ DE GUZMÁN, ANA CARO MALLÉN, AND SOR MARCELA DE SAN FÉLIX
Women Playwrights of Early Modern Spain
Edited by Nieves Romero-Díaz and Lisa Vollendorf
Translated and annotated by Harley Erdman
Volume 49, 2016

The Other Voice in
Early Modern Europe:
The Toronto Series

SERIES EDITORS Margaret L. King *and* Albert Rabil, Jr.
SERIES EDITOR, ENGLISH TEXTS Elizabeth H. Hageman

Previous Publications in the Series

ANNA TRAPNEL
Anna Trapnel's Report and Plea; or, A Narrative of Her Journey from London into Cornwall
Edited by Hilary Hinds
Volume 50, 2016

MARÍA VELA Y CUETO
Autobiography and Letters of a Spanish Nun
Edited by Susan Laningham
Translated by Jane Tar
Volume 51, 2016

CHRISTINE DE PIZAN
The Book of the Mutability of Fortune
Edited and translated by Geri L. Smith
Volume 52, 2017

MARGUERITE D'AUGE, RENÉE BURLAMACCHI, AND JEANNE DU LAURENS
Sin and Salvation in Early Modern France: Three Women's Stories
Edited, and with an introduction by Colette H. Winn. Translated by Nicholas Van Handel and Colette H. Winn
Volume 53, 2017

ISABELLA D'ESTE
Selected Letters
Edited and translated by Deanna Shemek
Volume 54, 2017

IPPOLITA MARIA SFORZA
Duchess and Hostage in Renaissance Naples: Letters and Orations
Edited and translated by Diana Robin and Lynn Lara Westwater
Volume 55, 2017

LOUISE BOURGEOIS
Midwife to the Queen of France: Diverse Observations
Translated by Stephanie O'Hara
Edited by Alison Klairmont Lingo
Volume 56, 2017

CHRISTINE DE PIZAN
Othea's Letter to Hector
Edited and translated by Renate Blumenfeld-Kosinski and Earl Jeffrey Richards
Volume 57, 2017

MARIE-GENEVIÈVE-CHARLOTTE THIROUX D'ARCONVILLE
Selected Philosophical, Scientific, and Autobiographical Writings
Edited and translated by Julie Candler Hayes
Volume 58, 2018

LADY MARY WROTH
Pamphilia to Amphilanthus *in Manuscript and Print*
Edited by Ilona Bell
Texts by Steven W. May and Ilona Bell
Volume 59, 2017

The Other Voice in
Early Modern Europe:
The Toronto Series

SERIES EDITORS Margaret L. King *and* Albert Rabil, Jr.
SERIES EDITOR, ENGLISH TEXTS Elizabeth H. Hageman

Previous Publications in the Series

Witness, Warning, and Prophecy: Quaker Women's Writing, 1655–1700
Edited by Teresa Feroli and Margaret Olofson Thickstun
Volume 60, 2018

Symphorien Champier
The Ship of Virtuous Ladies
Edited by Todd W. Reeser
Volume 61, 2018

Isabella Andreini
Mirtilla, A Pastoral: *A Bilingual Edition*
Edited by Valeria Finucci
Translated by Julia Kisacky
Volume 62, 2018

Margherita Costa
The Buffoons, A Ridiculous Comedy: *A Bilingual Edition*
Edited and translated by Sara E. Díaz and Jessica Goethals
Volume 63, 2018

Margaret Cavendish, Duchess of Newcastle
Poems and Fancies *with* The Animal Parliament
Edited by Brandie R. Siegfried
Volume 64, 2018

Margaret Fell
Women's Speaking Justified *and Other Pamphlets*
Edited by Jane Donawerth and Rebecca M. Lush
Volume 65, 2018

Mary Wroth, Jane Cavendish, and Elizabeth Brackley
Women's Household Drama:
Loves Victorie, A Pastorall, *and* The concealed Fansyes
Edited by Marta Straznicky and Sara Mueller
Volume 66, 2018

Eleonora Fonseca Pimentel
From Arcadia to Revolution: The Neapolitan Monitor *and Other Writings*
Edited and translated by Verina R. Jones
Volume 67, 2019

Charlotte Arbaleste Duplessis-Mornay, Anne de Chaufepié, and Anne Marguerite Petit Du Noyer
The Huguenot Experience of Persecution and Exile: Three Women's Stories
Edited by Colette H. Winn
Translated by Lauren King and Colette H. Winn
Volume 68, 2019

Anne Bradstreet
Poems and Meditations
Edited by Margaret Olofson Thickstun
Volume 69, 2019

ARCANGELA TARABOTTI

Antisatire: *In Defense of Women, against Francesco Buoninsegni*

Edited and translated by

ELISSA B. WEAVER

Iter Press
Toronto, Ontario

Arizona Center for Medieval and Renaissance Studies
Tempe, Arizona

2020

Iter Press
Tel: 416/978-7074 Email: iter@utoronto.ca
Fax: 416/978-1668 Web: www.itergateway.org

Arizona Center for Medieval and Renaissance Studies
Tel: 480/965-5900 Email: mrts@acmrs.org
Fax: 480/965-1681 Web: acmrs.org

Printed in Canada.

Library of Congress Cataloging-in-Publication Data

Names: Weaver, Elissa B., 1940– editor, translator. | Buoninsegni, Francesco, 1605–approximately 1660. Satira e antisatira. English. | Tarabotti, Arcangela. Antisatira. English.

Title: Arcangela Tarabotti : antisatire : in defense of women against Francesco Buoninsegni / edited and translated by Elissa B. Weaver.

Description: Toronto, Ontario : Iter Press ; Tempe, Arizona : Arizona Center for Medieval and Renaissance Studies, 2020. | Series: The other voice in early modern Europe. The Toronto series ; 70 | Includes bibliographical references and index. | Summary: "The English translation and study of the exchange of two seventeenth-century satires of women's and men's costume and comportment: the Sienese Francesco Buoninsegni's satire of the vanities of women, and the satirical response by the Venetian nun Arcangela Tarabotti, a defense of women and critique of the vanities of men"-- Provided by publisher.

Identifiers: LCCN 2019017432 (print) | LCCN 2019022109 (ebook) | ISBN 9780866986229 (paperback) | ISBN 9780866987554 (ebook)

Subjects: LCSH: Satire, Italian--Translations into English. | Fashion--Italy--History--17th century--Humor. | Italy--Social life and customs--17th century--Humor. | Buoninsegni, Francesco, 1605–approximately 1660. Satira e antisatira--Translations into English. | Tarabotti, Arcangela. Antisatira--Translations into English.

Classification: LCC PQ4053.S18 A73 2019 (print) | LCC PQ4053.S18 (ebook) | DDC 857/.509--dc23

LC record available at https://lccn.loc.gov/2019017432

LC ebook record available at https://lccn.loc.gov/2019022109

Cover illustration:
Detail from the *Concerto in Casa Lazzari* (seventeenth century) by Girolamo Martinelli. Musei di Palazzo dei Pio, Carpi.

Cover design:
Maureen Morin, Information Technology Services, University of Toronto Libraries.

Typesetting and production:
Iter Press.

Contents

Acknowledgments

My interest in the fascinating figure of Arcangela Tarabotti was first aroused by Ginevra Conti Odorisio's insightful studies of early Italian feminism (*Donna e società nel Seicento*, 1979, and *Storia dell'idea femminista in Italia*, 1980). In 1990 Francesca Medioli published Tarabotti's *Inferno monacale* whose manuscript she found in a private collection, and she added importantly to what was known of Tarabotti's life and writings. Meredith Ray and Lynn Westwater have carried on this work in an exemplary fashion, studying and publishing Tarabotti's letters and translating them for an English-speaking audience. They have now undertaken the formidable task of translating her *Paradiso monacale* and have illuminated many aspects of her life and her literary and social connections. I have learned much from their brilliant work and from our frequent collaboration. I owe them a great debt of thanks.

Other friends and colleagues helped me as I prepared the Italian edition of Tarabotti's *Antisatira* and Francesco Buoninsegni's *Satira menippea* and now my translation of those texts. First and foremost is Paolo Cherchi who has always been most generous with his erudition and without whose help I may never have recognized and understood some of Tarabotti's references to ancient texts. I thank Sharon Strocchia too for being my expert go-to source for historical information of many kinds, especially economic. I have been inspired by Gabriella Zarri's groundbreaking work on the history of female monasticism in Italy and on her studies of education and religious life in Italian convents, and I have profited from her advice and encouragement. I owe a special thanks to the late Phillip Gossett, a dear friend, who as Dean of Humanities at the University of Chicago in 1997 offered to support a small scholarly conference, the first of its kind devoted to the life and work of Arcangela Tarabotti; and I thank the University of Chicago Regenstein Library and the then director of Special Collections, Alice Schryer, for hosting a book exhibit in connection with the conference. I am very lucky to have had access to the vast resources of the Newberry Library and those of the Regenstein Library which have made it possible to study the context in which the Tarabotti-Buoninsegni debate took place without leaving Chicago. I began the research that led to this project many years ago at the Biblioteca Nazionale in Florence where I read the manuscript poetry of Francesco Buoninsegni; I thank the library for access to the treasures of their collections then and throughout the years.

I remember my good friend of many years, now greatly missed, Anne Jacobson Schutte, a brilliant historian who always willingly read with her critical eye and intelligence everything I submitted to her. I owe her thanks for improving my prose and an apology since I fear I could never meet her very high standards. Thanks too to Margaret King and Al Rabil for patiently waiting for me to finish this long-promised translation, and my copyeditor Amyrose McCue Gill and Margaret English-Haskin of Iter Press, whose assistance in putting the text into publishable form has been indispensable. I am also grateful to Bridget Madden, Margaret English-Haskin, and to Dott.ssa Tania Previdi and the Musei di Palazzo dei Pio di Carpi, Italy, for their generous help with my illustrations, and to the attentive reader of my manuscript for the correction she made and for her useful suggestions.

I dedicate this work to the memory of my father, John Owen Weaver, who taught me to love literature and languages. As a Protestant he had his reservations about Catholicism but I know he would have loved Arcangela Tarabotti as I do.

Illustrations

Introduction

> Men's bile, in short, is striving incessantly to employ sophistry with their lies against the female sex; they never stop blaming us for no other reason than envy, for since they cannot lord it over us by their merits, they must do so by their tongues.[1]

> And like Jove who struck down the giants with bolts of lightning, she with her *Antisatire* struck down Buoninsegni and other outsized intellects who dared to rise up against the female sex.[2]

A Strong Voice in Defense of Women

At a gathering in 1632 of the Academy of the Intronati in Siena and in the presence of the Grand Duke of Tuscany Ferdinando II de' Medici and members of his court, Francesco Buoninsegni, a prominent Sienese intellectual, delivered a semiserious discourse entitled *Contro 'l lusso donnesco, Satira menippea* (Against the Vanities of Women, a Menippean Satire) that denounced women's fashions as excessive ornamentation and an extraordinary waste of time and money. Menippean satire, an ancient literary form that had a revival in the late Renaissance, is a semiserious satire of ideas, conventions, and institutions written in a combination of prose and verse.[3] Buoninsegni's discourse also belongs to an age-old tradition of misogynist satires, which were popular in Italy during the sixteenth and seventeenth centuries when women's place in society was being widely debated and was a frequent topic of discourse in the literary academies.[4] Buoninsegni's satire was first published in

1. Arcangela Tarabotti, *Paternal Tyranny*, ed. and trans. Letizia Panizza (Chicago: University of Chicago Press, 2004), 134.

2. Giovanni Dandolo's letter to the signori Guerigli. Arcangela Tarabotti, *Letters Familiar and Formal*, ed. and trans. Meredith K. Ray and Lynn Lara Westwater (Toronto: Iter, Inc. and Centre for Reformation and Renaissance Studies, 2012), 49–50.

3. Menippean satire derives its name from the work of the Greek cynic philosopher Menippus of Gadara (third century BCE). The genre was introduced in Latin literature by Varro in the first century BCE. Justus Lipsius (1547–1606) revived the genre in the Renaissance. See the important catalogue of Menippean satires of the modern age: Eugene P. Kirk, *Menippean Satire: An Annotated Catalogue of Texts and Criticism* (New York: Garland Publishing, 1980).

4. Much has been written on this debate especially in the past fifty years. For an excellent overview see Ginevra Conti Odorisio's *Donne e società nel Seicento: Lucrezia Marinelli e Arcangela Tarabotti* (Rome: Bulzoni, 1979) and *Storia dell'idea femminista in Italia* (Turin: ERI, 1980), as well as Joan Kelly, "Early

Milan in 1637, according to Giammaria Mazzuchelli, but it seems no copy has survived.[5] It then appeared in Venice in 1638 with a polemical response written by Giovan Battista Torretti, a member of the Venetian Academy of the Incogniti.[6] Torretti's response seems to have garnered little interest and was soon forgotten.[7]

However, not long afterward—around 1641—Buoninsegni's satire came to the attention of the outspoken and spirited Venetian nun Arcangela Tarabotti, who decided to write a response—or, as she claims, was convinced by some important ladies to do so. Her work, the *Antisatira* (Antisatire) as it was called, was published in Venice together with Buoninsegni's satire in 1644 and created quite a furor and public outcry.[8] Tarabotti's response is not only a defense of women's

---

Feminist Theory and the *Querelle des Femmes*," in *Women, History, and Theory: The Essays of Joan Kelly* (Chicago: University of Chicago Press, 1984). See also the editors' introductions by Margaret L. King and Albert Rabil, Jr. to volumes of *The Other Voice in Early Modern Europe: The Chicago Series*. For the debate that flourished in response to Giuseppe Passi's *I donneschi difetti*—to which Tarabotti's works contributed—see Suzanne Magnanini and David Lamari, "Giuseppe Passi's Attacks on Women in 'The Defects of Women,'" in *In Dialogue with the Other Voice in Sixteenth-Century Italy: Literary and Social Contexts for Women's Writing*, ed. Julie D. Campbell and Maria Galli Stampino (Toronto: Iter Inc. and Centre for Reformation and Renaissance Studies, 2011), 143–94. On the subject of academy discussions, Giovanni Francesco Loredan mentions his speech to the Incogniti on the defects of women in a letter to Arcangela Tarabotti. See *Lettere del Signor Gio. Francesco Loredano, nobile veneto, divise in cinquantadue capi e raccolte da Henrico Giblet* [pseud. of Loredan] (Venice: Guerigli, 1657), 243–44. Ludovico Sesti, *Censura dell'Antisatira della signora Angelica* [sic] *Tarabotti fatta in risposta alla Satira menippea, Contro il lusso donnesco del sig. Franc. Buoninsegni scherzo geniale di Lucido Ossiteo* [pseud.] *accadem. aristocratico* (Siena: Bonetti, 1656), 117, acknowledges that many academic discourses of his day speak ill of women.

5. Francesco Buoninsegni, *Il lusso donnesco, Satira menippea* (Milan: Filippo Ghisolfi, 1637). See Giammaria Mazzuchelli, *Gli scrittori d'Italia, cioè Notizie storiche e critiche intorno alle vite e agli scritti dei letterati italiani*, vol. 2 (Brescia: Giambattista Bossini, 1763), 4:2398–2400, esp. 2399.

6. Francesco Buoninsegni, *Del lusso donnesco, Satira menippea … con l'Antisatira apologetica di Giovanni Battista Torretti* (Venice: Giacomo Sarzina, 1638). A brief biography of Torretti (active in the 1630s and 1640s) is found in the anonymous *Le glorie degli Incogniti, overo Gli hvomini illvstri dell'Accademia de' Signori Incogniti di Venetia* (Venice: Valvasense, 1647), 229–31; his portrait at age thirty-one is on page 228. Among his numerous published works are *Il leon corno panegirico … all'immortalità della Sereniss[im]a Republica di Venetia consecrato* (1635) and *La pietà trionfante panegirico … al serenissimo Ferdinando 2 il pio granduca di Toscana* (1636).

7. Torretti's response, solicited by Loredan, opens with a defense of women's beauty—a tour de force of Baroque conceits of description with which the author portrays the beauties of women. He defends their right to enhance their beauty through art and argues that husbands should be proud to see their worth displayed on their wives. He takes on Buoninsegni's other points as well—agreeing with some, disagreeing with others—but, after the rather spectacular conceits with which his response opens, the remainder seems perfunctory and obsequious.

8. *Contro 'l lusso donnesco, Satira menippea del Sig. Fran. Buoninsegni con l'Antisatira [di] D[onna] A[rcangela] T[arabotti] in risposta* (Venice: Francesco Valvasense, 1644). Valvasense published two editions in 1644, which I refer to as V1 and V2; another edition appeared in Siena in 1656 (see the

fashions and a denunciation of men, their clothes, and their hair styles but also a strong condemnation of men's treatment of women and, in general, of the subordination of women in society—central issues in all the writings of the talented literary nun. In this debate both Buoninsegni and Tarabotti write with the exaggeration and absurd arguments typical of Menippean satire; they show off their knowledge of ancient and contemporary literature in a prose style interspersed with poetry, as the genre required, and replete with the astonishing Baroque conceits that delighted their contemporaries. What perhaps most surprised the readers of this literary exchange and demands our attention today is that Tarabotti, an enclosed nun with only the rudimentary education available in the convent, displays a level of culture in no way inferior to that of her adversary—who had frequented the period's best institutions of learning as well as prestigious literary and scientific academies—and that she was not fooled by the supposedly semiserious nature of the academic discourse and in her response exposed its serious misogynist underpinnings.

The Protagonists of the Debate

Francesco Buoninsegni, a citizen of Siena and of the Grand Duchy of Tuscany, was born at the beginning of the seventeenth century and was still alive in 1655, when he is known to have recited a Latin elegy before the grand duke.[9] He studied in Rome at the Collegio Romano, first letters and philosophy, and later jurisprudence. When he returned to Siena, he served as secretary to Leopoldo de' Medici, then governor in the absence of his brother Mattias, who had been sent to lead the Tuscan army in Northern Italy and Germany. When Mattias returned to Siena, Buoninsegni entered his service. In Siena and Rome he frequented the academies, for which he wrote various discourses; he was also a member of the Venetian Academy of the Incogniti. In addition to his satire of women's fashions, he later wrote another in which he denounced the foolishness of men. He is also the author of an elegy in Latin on the death of an elephant and a meditation on the stigmata of Saint Catherine of Siena; he wrote sonnets, especially occasional poetry, some on scientific topics such as the clock, the silkworm, and astronomical discoveries.[10]

Note on the Text and Translation). The modern edition is Francesco Buoninsegni and Arcangela Tarabotti, *Satira e Antisatira*, ed. Elissa Weaver (Rome: Salerno Editrice, 1998). References to this edition of the *Satira* appear as Buoninsegni, *Satira* (Weaver) and to this edition of the *Antisatira* as Tarabotti, *Antisatira* (Weaver).

9. On Buoninsegni's life, see the entry by Martino Capucci, *Dizionario biografico degli italiani* (Rome: Instituto dell'Enciclopedia Italiana, 1972), 15:254–55, and *Le glorie degli Incogniti*, 149–51; his portrait at age forty-three is on page 148. See also Mazzuchelli, *Gli scrittori d'Italia*, vol. 2, 4:2398–2400.

10. Two copies of *Delle sciocchezze degli huomini* (The foolishness of men) are found in Florence at the Biblioteca Nazionale Centrale (BNCF), Magl. VII 456: a fair copy on fols. 53r–84r and an incomplete

Arcangela Tarabotti was born on February 24, 1604 to Stefano Tarabotti and Maria Cadena dei Tolentini in the section of Venice known as Castello;[11] she was baptized Elena Cassandra.[12] The family, if not of the citizen class, was certainly of considerable means. Elena was the fifth of their ten children, the eldest of seven daughters. Two of her sisters married: Innocenza Elisabetta to Francesco Dario, the family doctor, and Lorenzina to the lawyer Giacomo Pighetti. Four sisters, Camilla Angela, Angela Lorenza, Lucia Caterina, and Caterina Agnese remained at home, while Elena was destined for the religious life, perhaps because she was the least likely to marry, being born with a limp and having somewhat precarious health. At the age of eleven, as she writes, or thirteen, as convent documents attest, she entered the Benedictine convent of Sant'Anna, a fate she deplored. Nevertheless, she was clothed in 1620, taking Arcangela as her religious name, professed in 1623, and was consecrated in 1629. She died on February 28, 1652, at the age of forty-eight. Arcangela Tarabotti did not have a religious vocation but had to submit to the will of her family; she made protesting the practice of forced

---

autograph copy on fols. 97r–109v. The opening quatrains of the *Sciocchezze* (fols. 55v–57v) refer to the earlier satire against the vanities of women and the negative reaction Buoninsegni had received from women. On his literary production see also Roser Melchor i Fenollosa, "Sonets esparsos de Francesco Buoninsegni" (PhD diss., University of Valencia, 2005), which includes an edition of thirty sonnets and a general overview of his opus. Poetry by Buoninsegni is found in the following manuscript collections, also at the BNCF: Magl. VII, 357, 359, 369, 456; and Palatino 263, 248, 268.

11. Stefano Tarabotti was a chemist, perhaps involved in the production of paints: see Mario Infelise, "Books and Politics in Arcangela Tarabotti's Venice," in *Arcangela Tarabotti: A Literary Nun in Baroque Venice*, ed. Elissa B. Weaver (Ravenna: Longo, 2006), 57, and note 1. This chapter also appeared in Italian as Mario Infelise, "Libri e politica nella Venezia di Arcangela Tarabotti," *Annali di storia moderna e contemporanea*, 8 (2002): 32–45.

12. I take the details of her life from the biography by Emilio Zanette, *Suor Arcangela: Monaca del Seicento veneziano* (Venice: Istituto per la collaborazione culturale, 1960), updated with Arcangela Tarabotti, *L'"Inferno monacale" di Arcangela Tarabotti*, ed. Francesca Medioli (Turin: Rosenberg & Sellier, 1990), esp. 109–92 ("Chiavi di lettura"); Medioli, "Alcune lettere autografe di Arcangela Tarabotti: Autocensura e immagine di sé," *Rivista di storia e letteratura religiosa* 32 (1996): 133–55; Medioli, "Arcangela Tarabotti's Reliability about Herself: Publication and Self-Representation (Together with a Small Collection of Previously Unpublished Letters)," *The Italianist* 23 (2003): 54–101; and Medioli, "Des liaisons dangereuses? Réseaux hérités, supposés et déguisés d'une nonne vénitienne au XVIIe siècle," *Genre & Histoire* 11 (Fall 2012) <http://journals.openedition.org/genrehistoire/1750>. I have also consulted Natalia Costa-Zalessow, "La condanna all''Indice' della 'Semplicità ingannata' di Arcangela Tarabotti alla luce di manoscritti inediti," *Nouvelles de la république des lettres* 1 (2002): 97–113; Margherita Valenti, "Sant'Anna di Castello. Inventario archivistico di un monastero benedettino femminile" (PhD diss., University of Venice, Ca' Foscari, 2005/2006), esp. 22–30; Meredith K. Ray, "Letters and Lace: Arcangela Tarabotti and Convent Culture in Seicento Venice," in *Early Modern Women and Transnational Communities of Letters*, ed. Julie Campbell and Ann Larsen (Aldershot, Farnham, Surrey, UK: Ashgate, 2009), 45–73; and Lynn L. Westwater, "A Rediscovered Friendship in the Republic of Letters: The Unpublished Correspondence of Arcangela Tarabotti and Ismaël Boulliau," *Renaissance Quarterly* 65, no. 1 (2012): 67–134.

monachization and, more generally, the denial to women of free will the driving passion of her life. There is no doubt that she hoped through her writing to effect change, if only in the minds of men, and that she should be considered an early feminist thinker and activist.

Convents in Italy by the sixteenth and seventeenth centuries had become the home of a large percentage of women of the elite and merchant classes; they were a safe, respectable, often prestigious place for the daughters for whom families could not find appropriate marriage partners. Many factors went into the decision, but it was always the family that decided and rarely, if ever, the daughters. The considerations were many, primarily economic and social. Convent dowries were much lower than those required for marriage, and when a daughter entered religious life she renounced all claim to her family's fortunes, which would be handed down through one heir and the patrimony preserved. There was also the important concern of maintaining family prestige only through marriages that reinforced or improved a family's social standing; and, certainly a girl's physical endowments, her appearance and health, were factored importantly into the decision. There were many women, too, who had a religious calling and who chose to live their lives in prayer in a community where they prepared for the next life and earned respect here for their contributions to their families and society. It is difficult to know, however, who of these were the truly willing and who understood that there was no alternative available to them. The church, in the years following the Council of Trent, made free consent a requirement, but did not and generally could not support reluctant women (or men) if their decisions contradicted those of their families. Many convent women protested, claiming to be "prisoners," and often exacting privileges in exchange for acceptance of their situation. Arcangela Tarabotti spent her life denouncing her incarceration and she took up the defense of all women who, like her, were unwilling nuns.[13]

13. Much has been written on the subject since the early nineteenth century when Alessandro Manzoni created the unforgettable character of the forced nun Gertrude in his novel *I promessi sposi* (The Betrothed, 1827), inspired by the seventeenth-century trial of Suor Virginia Maria de Leyva, the so-called "nun of Monza." Most contemporary studies take their initial inspiration from the work of Gabriella Zarri and especially her seminal essay "Monasteri femminili e città, secoli XV–XVIII," in *Storia d'Italia: Annali*, vol. 9: *La Chiesa e il potere politico dal Medioevo all'età contemporanea*, ed. Giorgio Chittolini and Giovanni Miccoli (Turin: Einaudi, 1986), 357–429. See also Zarri, "Monasteri femminili in Italia nel secolo XVI," in Gabriella Zarri, Francesca Medioli, and Paola Vismarra Chiappa, "'De monialibus,' secoli XVI–XVII–XVIII," *Rivista di storia e letteratura religiosa* 33 (1997): 643–69; and Francesca Medioli, "Monacazioni forzate: Donne ribelli al proprio destino," *Clio: Trimestrale di studi storici* 30 (1994): 431–54; and on Venice, Jutta Sperling, *Convents and the Body Politic in Late Renaissance Venice* (Chicago: University of Chicago Press, 1999), 18–71. An excellent, well-documented account of forced monachization, male and female, is found in Anne Jacobson Schutte, *By Force and Fear: Taking and Breaking Monastic Vows in Early Modern Europe* (Ithaca, NY: Cornell University Press, 2011).

The convent, it must be said, allowed Tarabotti—however much she rightfully protested—to live a life of study and writing that would not have been so easily hers had she remained in the secular world. In the convent she had time to devote to her studies since she was exempt from holding convent offices. It was not uncommon for families who could afford it to pay the convent for an exemption for their daughters, often a way of acknowledging their social rank but perhaps, in Tarabotti's case, because of her intellectual interests and ability—and to make it less painful for her to accept her condition. She also had the privilege of writing and receiving letters without the oversight of the convent abbess and she could receive visitors of her choosing and converse with them at the grate in the convent parlor.

Tarabotti would have learned to read and write at home before entering the convent of Sant'Anna, where, if we can take her at her word, she learned little more from convent teachers. She claims to be entirely self-taught. Society's failure to educate women was a subject about which she was passionate and to which she returns frequently in her writing. In one of the digressions in the *Antisatira*, she explains that most of her learning has come from "reading good books, both religious and profane, Latin and vernacular, through which, however crudely, and without anyone to teach me, I have somewhat smoothed out the roughness of my intellect" (69).[14] In her letters she often discusses her access to books and makes it clear that she read widely.[15] To her critics who accuse her of writing without art and order (which in fact is not the case), she responds that she prefers to be guided by her caprice rather than by the rules of rhetoric and that her talent is a gift from God.[16]

It was probably through her brother-in-law Giacomo Pighetti, a member of the Venetian Academy of the Incogniti, that Tarabotti was introduced to members of the Venetian literary and publishing world and her voice reached an audience beyond the walls of Sant'Anna. Her contacts with the secular world also extended to members of the French diplomatic representation in Venice, to their wives and children, and to many men and women of elite society who corresponded with her and who visited her at the convent. Her correspondence, much of which she

14. All in-text page references are to the present edition of the *Satire* and *Antisatire*. References in the notes to the present edition appear as follows: Buoninsegni, *Satire* [page(s)]; Tarabotti, *Antisatire* [page(s)]. Translations of quoted texts, unless otherwise noted, are mine throughout.

15. Tarabotti often refers to an exchange of books with friends in the Academy of the Incogniti. In a letter to Girolamo Brusoni, commenting on his novel *Orestilla*, she writes that she reads everything that appears in print and has read the best books of the greatest thinkers—even Machiavelli—with the permission of her superiors. She seems pleased that, in the *Orestilla*, suor Laura, a forced nun, is a scarcely disguised version of herself. See Tarabotti, *Letters*, 250–51 (letter 213).

16. For an excellent, detailed analysis of Tarabotti's style and language, see Simona Bortot, "Introduzione: La penna all'ombra delle grate," in Tarabotti, *La semplicità ingannata: Edizione critica e commentata*, ed. Simona Bortot (Padua: Il Poligrafo, 2007), 138–47.

published, attests to her many friends and associates—and also to difficult as well as friendly relations with some among them, especially with several members of the Incogniti. These were writers whose support she could not always count upon, some of whom would betray her trust—like the itinerant friar and book collector Angelico Aprosio, who wrote against her, and the prolific novelist Girolamo Brusoni, whose friendship with her ended in a literary dispute.[17] Giovan Francesco Loredan, a prominent member of Venetian society, the founder of the Venetian Academy of the Incogniti, and a power in Venetian publishing at the time, was a continued influence in her literary career. He admired her talent and, in the exaggerated literary style of the period, he wrote in a letter to her that "the world has become a theater of the marvels of your pen!"[18] He helped her publish several of her works, though his misogyny was often a subject of disagreement between them.

It was undoubtedly the libertine bent of many of the Incogniti that attracted their attention to such an outspoken nun, and their common intellectual interests that caused them to take notice of her intelligence and her protest. They were freethinkers, disdainful of dogmas and conventional morality; their work and lives were characterized by scandal and impertinence.[19] Prominent figures in the

17. Angelico Aprosio (1607–1681), known as "il Ventimiglia," was an Augustinian friar, itinerant book collector, and the member of several academies, including the Academy of the Incogniti. See the entry on Aprosio by Alberto Asor-Rosa, *Dizionario biografico degli italiani*, 3 (1961): 650–53, and the more recent study in Quinto Marini, "Angelico Aprosio da Ventimiglia 'tromba per far conoscer molti,'" in *Frati barocchi: Studi su A. G. Brignole Sale, G. A. De Marini, A. Aprosio, F. F. Frugoni, P. Segneri* (Modena: Mucchi, 2000), 153–79, at 170–76 for his relationship with Tarabotti. Girolamo Brusoni (1614–after 1686) was a prolific writer, ex-Carthusian monk, and libertine, who in his early career was known especially for his novels. He was a member of the Incogniti and for a time a friend and correspondent of Tarabotti. He angered Tarabotti by using her work in his novel *Le turbolenze delle vestali* (written between 1640 and 1642) and he wrote the *Antisatira satirizzata* (1645), which may never have been published; Tarabotti considered it the best of the responses to her *Antisatira*. Tarabotti, *Letters*, 151 (letter 99). On Brusoni, see Zanette, *Suor Arcangela*, 132–34, 277, and Gaspare De Caro, "Girolamo Brusoni," in *Dizionario biografico degli italiani*, 14 (1972): 712–20.

18. "La carriera delle lodi di V. S. non dee restringersi in questo foglio; già che il mondo l'è divenuto Teatro delle maraviglie della sua penna." See Loredano, *Lettere*, 431. Giovanni Francesco Loredan (1606–1661) was a member of the Venetian nobility and a senator of the Venetian Republic. In 1630 he founded the Academy of the Incogniti. He was a prolific writer of, among many other works, *Degli scherzi geniali* (1632), *La Dianea* (1635), *Bizzarrie academiche* (1638), *L'Adamo* (1640), *Novelle amorose* (1643, 1651), and his *Lettere* (1657). He also wrote plays and published an edition of Giovan Battista Marino's *Lira* (1633). Loredan dedicated the third part of his novel *Hibraino* to Tarabotti. See Loredano, *Lettere*, 435; see also Letizia Panizza, "Volume Editor's Introduction," in Tarabotti, *Paternal Tyranny*, 8n16.

19. On the libertine character of members of the Academy of the Incogniti, see Giorgio Spini, *Ricerca dei libertini: La teoria dell'impostura delle religioni nel Seicento italiano* (Florence: La Nuova Italia, 1983), 145–76. On Loredan's influence on the Venetian press, see Mario Infelise, "Ex ignotus notus? Note sul tipografo Sarzina e l'Accademia degli Incogniti," in *Libri, tipografi, biblioteche: Ricerche*

literary scene in Venice at the time, they read her work and shared it with others.[20] Yet Tarabotti's relationship with these and other members of the Academy of the Incogniti, as a recent critic has put it, was characterized by "a precarious equilibrium, in which sincere appreciation and demonstrations of esteem existed alongside an impossible divide that separated the fierce and unmitigated misogyny of the members of the academy and the feminist assertions of the nun."[21]

Tarabotti's first work, probably begun shortly after her entrance at Sant'Anna, was a polemical treatise in three books initially entitled *Tirannia paterna* (*Paternal Tyranny*). In it she accuses men of incarcerating women in convents out of avarice and pride; she denounces the state for encouraging the practice in order to limit the size of the nobility and the church for failing to uphold the decrees of the Council of Trent against forced monachization and for not permitting the involuntary religious to dissolve their vows. She argues for the education of women and their participation in public life; she decries the misogyny of men and their cruel treatment of women, which men justify by insistence on female inferiority and necessary subjection. She extolls the virtues of women and argues that the world would recognize their superiority were they allowed an education.

Tarabotti claims to have written the treatise over a period of nine months while she recovered from a bout of the illness that plagued her throughout her life, but she returned to the work again and again over the years, making changes to it as late as 1644. She renamed it *La Semplicità ingannata* (Innocence deceived), perhaps hoping to improve her chances for publication, but her outspoken criticism of specific individuals, the church, and the state proved to be too great an obstacle for publication in Italy. She had hopes to publish it in France but they too were frustrated. Despite these setbacks, she persisted until she found persons sympathetic to her cause and a publisher out of the reach of the Roman Church: in the last two years of her life she had the satisfaction of learning that printing

---

storiche dedicate a Luigi Balsamo, ed. Arnaldo Ganda (Florence: Olschki, 1997), 207–23, and Infelise, "Books and Politics."

20. Bissari read the *Antisatira* to members of the Academy Olimpica in Vicenza; Buoninsegni to friends in the academy in Siena. For her renown in Vicenza, see Pietro Paolo Bissari, *Le scorse olimpiche, trattenimenti accademici* (Venice: Francesco Valvasense, 1648), 12–13, 190–91. Bissari calls her "quella divina Tarabotta, anzi terremoto, … pregio delle donne, rossor de gli huomini, portento delle virtù, stupor del sesso, miracolo dell'età" (that divine Tarabotti, indeed an upheaval on earth … pride of womankind, an embarrassment for men, a wonder of virtue, a marvel of her sex, a miracle of the age). Bissari, *Le scorse*, 190–91. For Siena, see Giuseppe Portigliotti, *Penombre claustrali* (Milan: Fratelli Treves, 1930), 285.

21. "un precario equilibrio, in cui i sinceri apprezzamenti e le dimostrazioni di stima si affiancarono a un'incolmabile frattura tra la feroce ed esasperata misoginia degli accademici e le rivendicazioni femminili della monaca." Emanuela Bufacchi, "'La mia semplicità è stata ingannata dalla sagacia del serpente': Polemiche di Girolamo Brusoni con Arcangela Tarabotti," *Esperienze letterarie* 40, no. 2 (2015): 61.

was underway with the Elzevir Press in Leiden (Netherlands), but she died in 1652—two years before the book appeared.[22] In 1661 it was condemned by the Holy Office and placed on the *Index of Forbidden Books*.[23]

Another work that would not appear during her lifetime—indeed not until it was rediscovered by Francesca Medioli and published in 1990—was a scathing treatise entitled *Inferno monacale* (Convent Hell) in which Tarabotti compared life in the convent to tragic theater and to hell on earth.[24] She mentions another work, *Purgatorio delle malmaritate* (Purgatory of unhappily married women), which was to be part of a Dantean trilogy together with *Inferno monacale* and with her first published work, *Paradiso monacale* (*Convent Paradise*). If she actually wrote the *Purgatorio* it has been lost, but much of what surely would have comprised it can be found in her defense of women in the *Antisatira*. In her letters she mentions four other works that have been lost: three on religious subjects—the *Contemplazioni dell'anima amante* (Contemplations of the loving soul), the *Via lastricata per andare al cielo* (Paved road to Heaven), and *Luce monacale* (Convent light)—and a play entitled *Ardire, comedia* (Boldness, a comedy).[25]

22. *La Semplicità ingannata di Galerana Baratotti* [pseud.] (Leiden: Gio. Sambix [Elzevir], 1654). Late in the publishing process Tarabotti wrote to Ismaël Boulliau, who was seeing the book to press, asking to entitle it *La tirannia paterna, overo Semplicità ingannata di Galerana Barcitotti consacrata a Dio*, but her request must have arrived too late. See Westwater, "A Rediscovered Friendship," 69–70, 70n9, 71 fig. 1, 74 fig. 3. There was a second edition bearing the same title, date, and place of publication, but entirely reset and probably printed in Venice. For a description of the two editions, see Simona Bortot's "Nota al testo" to her edition of the *Semplicità ingannata*, 155–62.

23. Costa-Zalessow ("La condanna all'"Indice'") provides the full text of the Holy Office's *censura* in Latin with commentary in Italian; she includes two lists of objections to the work made by examiners in Natalia Costa-Zalessow, "Tarabotti's 'La semplicità ingannata' and Its Twentieth-Century Interpreters, with Unpublished Documents Regarding Its Condemnation to the 'Index,'" *Italica* 78 (2001): 320–21. Panizza ("Volume Editor's Introduction," in Tarabotti, *Paternal Tyranny*, 27–29) provides a summary of the accusations and, in her notes, direct quotations from some of the Latin documents.

24. Tarabotti, *L'"Inferno monacale."* On this text see also Nicoletta Lissoni, "La 'ragion di stato' monacale nel pensiero di Arcangela Tarabotti," in *Amazzoni, sante, ninfe, variazioni di storia delle idee dall'antichità al Rinascimento*, ed. Davide Bigalli (Milan: Cortina, 2006), 247–60, and Nancy L. Canepa, "The Writing Behind the Wall: Arcangela Tarabotti's 'Inferno monacale' and Cloistral Autobiography in the Seventeenth Century," *Forum italicum* 30 (1996): 1–23.

25. In a letter Tarabotti tells her friend Betta Polani that she is sending her these three works which she may publish, if she sees fit: "Le *Contemplazioni dell'anima amante* (Contemplations of the loving soul), la *Via lasciata del cielo* (The Road to Heaven Abandoned), e la *Luce monacale* (Convent light) siano stampate, se cosí piace a Voi." Tarabotti, *Letters*, 82–83 (letter 26). The title of the second of these works appears in a different form in the letter to the signori Guerigli that introduces Tarabotti's letter collection. This letter, written by Giovanni Dandolo (1613–1661), a Venetian aristocrat, friend of Tarabotti, and her frequent correspondent, instead cites her work as the *Via lastricata per andare al cielo* (Paved road to Heaven). Tarabotti, *Letters*, 49–50. Dandolo's version fits better in this group of works, and "lasciata" could be a typesetter's error for "lastricata," but ultimately both titles are plausible. In a letter addressed to her friend the French ambassador Nicolo Bretel de Gremonville, she claims to be writing

Tarabotti published five works during her lifetime. The first two, in 1643—but with the erroneous date, clearly a typographical error, of 1663—were *Paradiso monacale*, published in Venice by Guglielmo Oddoni, and prefaced to it a *Soliloquio a Dio* (*Soliloquy to God*).[26] The *Soliloquio* is a confession of her sinful state and a prayer for forgiveness and help. *Paradiso monacale*, perhaps because it follows such a *Soliloquio* and extolls convent life for those who have a religious vocation, has been seen by many of Tarabotti's early scholars as a retraction of her prior writing, but it is not. In it she defends her earlier work, claiming that what she wrote in *Tirannia paterna* and *Inferno monacale*, if perhaps she "let [her] pen go a bit too far," was a "truthful depiction of reality."[27] We should more likely read the inclusion and the position of the *Soliloquio* as a necessary subterfuge that made it possible for Tarabotti to get a work of hers in print—a work that would be deemed an appropriate literary debut for a nun.[28] She indeed makes a strong defense of convent life in *Paradiso monacale*, but only for those women who have a religious calling, whom she distinguishes from those who have been forced. While she is less outspoken in her criticism of men than usual, she opens the treatise with the words "God loves all creatures but especially woman, and then man though he does not deserve it."[29] In 1644 her *Antisatira* appeared in Venice, published by Francesco Valvasense together with Francesco Buoninsegni's *Satira*.[30] In 1651, with *Che le donne siano della spetie degli huomini* (*Women Are of the Human Species*), she responded to an even more outlandish misogynist tract that argued that women had no souls and did not belong to humankind. Originally

---

a play, the *Ardire, comedia*, in response to Angelico Aprosio's attack, the *Maschera scoperta*, whose publication, however, she was able to suppress. Tarabotti, *Letters*, 151–52 (letter 99).

26. Arcangela Tarabotti, *Il Paradiso monacale, libri tre, con un soliloquio a Dio* (Venice: Guglielmo Oddoni, 1643). The *Soliloquio* appears on pages 1–34 of this edition. *Convent Paradise*, an English translation by Ray and Westwater, is forthcoming in the Other Voice Series; it includes the *Soliloquy*.

27. Both passages appear in the opening message to her *Lettore* (Reader), where she states that *Tirannia paterna* and *Inferno monacale* are "filled with observations that are real and truthful" (ripieni di sensi reali e verdadieri) and that she should not be criticized because, she writes, "I let my pen go a bit too far in defense of my sex" (ho lasciato trascorrere un poco con la penna a difesa del mio sesso). Tarabotti, *Il Paradiso monacale*, 39. See also Tarabotti, *Letters*, 99–100 (letter 44): "[O]ne who is not in love with God cannot speak of him. I was much better able to describe *Paternal Tyranny* and to erect the workings of *Inferno* than to describe the greatness of *Paradise*." (Non sa parlare di Dio chi non è innamorato di Dio. Molto meglio ho saputo ispiegare la *Tirannia paterna* e inalzare una machina d'*Inferno* che descrivere la mole di *Paradiso*). Tarabotti, *Lettere*, 101.

28. For Medioli the *Soliloquio* is a "fictitious account of this supposed conversion," Tarabotti's attempt "to make her literary image acceptable." Medioli, "Arcangela Tarabotti's Reliability," 55; see 92n5 for a list of the early critics who read it as a conversion.

29. Tarabotti, *Il Paradiso monacale*, 41: "Iddio Benedetto ama tutte le creature, ma particolarmente la donna, e poi l'huomo, benché egli non lo meriti."

30. See note 8 above.

published in Germany, it was translated into Italian by a fictitious Oratio Plata (thought to be Loredan), who called it a *Disputatio perjucunda* (Most delightful disputation).[31] Tarabotti found it offensive and heretical. In 1650 she published her *Lettere familiari e di complimento* (*Letters Familiar and Formal*) together with a lament for the death of a friend, *Le Lagrime d'Arcangela Tarabotti per la morte dell'illustrissima Signora Regina Donati* (*The Tears of Arcangela Tarabotti upon the Death of the Most Illustrious Signora Regina Donati*).[32] The letters provide information about her daily life in the convent, her precarious health, and her contacts with the secular world. They document her attempts to publish (especially the *Antisatira*) and to defend her literary reputation from critics who argued that she must have had help to write her works.

For Tarabotti, her writing was her life. To her friend Betta Polani, who warned her that it was ruining her health, Tarabotti responded: "that I should not be writing is quite impossible. In this prison and in my illness nothing else will satisfy me .... If I had not this diversion, I would be dead by now ... only a tempered pen can temper my suffering."[33]

It seems incredible today that a nun at that time could publish a collection of private letters, since convent women were forbidden to correspond with anyone other than members of their immediate family, and with them only with the consent of the convent prioress or abbess.[34] Tarabotti seems to have had permission

31. *Che le donne siano della spetie degli huomini: Difesa della donna di Galerana Barcitotti* [pseud.] *contra Horatio Plata il traduttore di quei fogli che dicono le donne non essere della spetie degli huomini* (Nuremberg: Iuvan Cherchenbergher [fictitious place and publisher], 1651) was Tarabotti's response to *Che le donne non siano della spetie degli huomini: Discorso piacevole tradotto da Oratio Plata romano* (Lyon: Per Gasparo Ventura [but Venice: Francesco Valvasense], 1647). For the actual publisher of this text, see Infelise, "Books and Politics," 67–69. The original work was published ca. 1595 in Germany without either place or date of publication, but probably in Leipzig by the Osthaus press, and attributed to Valens Acidalius. According to Giorgio Spini (*Ricerca dei libertini*, 222), Loredan sold copies in his house of the Italian translation of the tract, which he called a *Disputatio perjucunda*. There is a modern edition and a translation of this exchange: Arcangela Tarabotti, *Che le donne siano della spezie degli uomini: Women are No Less Rational Than Men*, ed. Letizia Panizza (London: Institute of Romance Studies, 1994), and *"Women are Not Human": An Anonymous Treatise and Responses*, ed. and trans. Theresa M. Kenney (New York: Crossroad Publishing, 1998). *Women Are of the Human Species*, the translation of Tarabotti's response, is on pages 87–159.

32. *Lettere familiari e di complimento* and *Le Lagrime d'Arcangela Tarabotti per la morte dell'illustrissima Signora Regina Donati* (Venice: Guerigli, 1650). The text of *Le Lagrime* follows the letters on pages 323–84 of this edition. The English translation by Ray and Westwater, *Letters Familiar and Formal*, includes an excerpt from the *The Tears of Arcangela Tarabotti upon the Death of the Most Illustrious Signora Regina Donati* on pages 285–96; a full edition is forthcoming.

33. Tarabotti, *Letters*, 103–104 (letter 49). I have slightly altered the translation, substituting "not be" for "leave off."

34. For a list of regulations restricting the letter writing of nuns, see the "Introduction" to Tarabotti, *Letters*, 20–21.

to do so without the oversight of her superiors.[35] These were extraordinary times in Venice. Had she lived later in the century, it is unlikely that she would have enjoyed the freedom she had to communicate with the outside world and to associate with members of the Academy of the Incogniti, or to publish polemical works like the *Antisatira* and *Che le donne siano della spetie degli huomini*, which, like her letter collection, appeared in Venice.

In the first half of the seventeenth century, relations were difficult between the Venetian Republic and the Holy See. Venice had been put under the interdict by Pope Paul V in 1606 in a complex dispute over local versus papal control in matters secular and ecclesiastical. Venice asserted its independence of Rome, its so-called "libertà veneziana," in many ways. They expelled the Jesuits, then the Capuchins and Theatines, and they sent the apostolic nuncio back to Rome. For a while they successfully kept inquisitional interference in check.[36] In the 1630s, 1640s, and 1650s, the Venetians themselves and the Riformatori in Padua decided what could be published and what not, and members of the Academy of the Incogniti, many of whom were hostile to any form of religion, were responsible for almost half of what was published in Venice. The most powerful figure in Venetian publishing then was Tarabotti's patron and friend Giovan Francesco Loredan.[37]

It was a time when even works that could not be officially acknowledged were allowed to appear in Venetian terretory with false publishing information. This was true, for example, of the exchange between Tarabotti and the author/translator of the German tract that claimed that women had no souls. Both texts purported to have been published outside of Venice. Tarabotti's response appeared as Galerana Barcitotti, *Che le donne siano della spetie degli huomini: Difesa della donna* (Nuremberg: Iuvann Cherchenbergher, 1651), but it was published in Venice by Francesco Valvasense, a favorite of the Incogniti whose work was supported by Loredan. Tarabotti's *Antisatira*, too, had been published by Valvasense in 1644. Only a few years later, when relations between Venice and the Roman Church were repaired—when Venice needed the assistance of the papacy in its war in Candia—was there a radical change in the Venetian Republic's policies toward the Holy See and a rapprochement between the two states.[38] The Jesuits were allowed to return in 1657. Some of the freedoms the Republic had enjoyed earlier were curtailed, among them the freedom to publish controversial texts.[39]

35. Valenti, "Sant'Anna di Castello," 28.

36. Infelise, "Books and Politics," 57–72, and see his note 2 on studies of politics and culture in seventeenth-century Venice.

37. Infelise, "Books and Politics," 58.

38. Infelise, "Books and Politics," esp. 66.

39. Infelise, "Books and Politics," 66–72.

Satire and Antisatire

Francesco Buoninsegni intended to entertain his audience with a humorous denunciation of contemporary ladies' fashions. According to Angelico Aprosio, among those present at Buoninsegni's performance were the Grand Duke Ferdinando II de' Medici, the Medici princes Mattias and Leopoldo, and many members of the Florentine and Sienese nobility, including women.[40] Buoninsegni did not hesitate to criticize gentlewomen (though in jest, he insists) for squandering their families' fortunes in pursuit of the latest fashions, even though some (many?) women were among his audience. They did so out of ignorance, he argues, and disregard for the waste of treasure. He ridicules their elaborate hairstyles and admonishes them for the excess of rich fabric required for the extra length of dress needed to cover them because of their high platform shoes. The humor of his discourse consists of bizarre analogies, extended Baroque conceits, and curious anecdotes. He compares women's enormous fashionable hairdos to a deck of Tarot cards and then describes the hair and comportment of ladies in terms of the various suits of Italian and French playing cards: "Coins (*denari*) are there but ill spent .... Swords (*spade*) are not lacking; every woman so that she looks like Pallas ... must have her little silver sword. Clubs (*bastoni*) are worn hidden beneath the curls" (50). His analogies are preposterous, yet they would seem to have been suggested by some of the more elaborate coiffures that were in style (see figs. 1 and 2). He argues that, high on their wooden platform shoes adorned in gold and silver, women appear to be frightening and precarious statues, ready to crash to the ground like the one in the dream of the biblical Nebuchadnezzar.[41] He fears that their hard wooden shoes could serve as a weapon to be used against men. He calls women's silk gowns "worms" (*vermi*) because of the origin of the fabric, and their hair and wigs the grotesque remains of the dead, since wigs were often made from the hair of corpses.

40. According to Angelico Aprosio in *La Maschera scoperta*, "[t]hose in whose presence the Discourse was recited were the Most Serene Grand Duke Ferdinando II, our prince, with the Most Serene princes, the brothers Mattias and Leopoldo, besides Florentine and Sienese nobility, who all rushed there together. There were ladies too ...." (Coloro alla presenza de' quali fu recitato il Discorso, furono il Serenissimo Gran Duca Ferdinando II nostro Principe con li Serenissimi Principi fratelli Mattias, e Leopoldo, oltre la nobilità Fiorentina, e Sanese, che vi concorsero a gara. Non vi mancarono le Dame). Later he adds "There were women and even women writers: Signora Cammilla Martini da Nizza along with our Signora Lucretia Mignanelli" (Ce ne sono state, e pur ce ne sono delle letterate: e la Signora Cammilla Martini da Nizza, con la nostra Signora Lucretia Mignanelli). See the modern edition of Aprosio's work edited by Emilia Biga in her *Una polemica antifemminista del '600: "La maschera scoperta" di Anglico Aprosio* (Ventimiglia: Civica Biblioteca Aprosiana, 1989), 124–25.

41. Daniel 2:31–35.

Figure 1. Seventeenth century women's hair style, from *Recueil général des coiffures depuis 1589* (Paris: Desnos, 1778). Courtesy of the Newberry Library, Chicago, Illinois.

Figure 2. Seventeenth century women's hair style, from *Recueil général des coiffures depuis 1589* (Paris: Desnos, 1778). Courtesy of the Newberry Library, Chicago, Illinois.

Buoninsegni's text is replete with proverbs and allusions to ancient literature and lore, often invented—as, for instance, his claim that women are like flies since neither women nor flies were allowed in the temple of Hercules. There is no clear development to the discourse overall but Buoninsegni gives it a superficial structure by beginning and ending it with protests of innocence (he was forced to speak against women) and fear (they might retaliate, as the Maenads did against Orpheus). His satire is interspersed with poetry; some poems are his own, but it is a stretch that he compares his poetic prowess to that attributed to the Orpheus of myth. Perhaps this exaggeration was meant to amuse his audience. Indeed, he opens his discourse allying himself—here, too, incongruously—with the most famous poet of the Italian Renaissance, using as his own excuse the disclaimer of Ludovico Ariosto, who begins canto twenty-eight of the *Orlando furioso* asking his audience not to take seriously the misogynist account he is about to relate.[42]

Buoninsegni shows off his learning by citing from classical and contemporary poets: Martial, Ovid, Petrarch, Ariosto, Battista Guarini, and others whom he does not identify, one of whom he claims to be a woman poet. He cites his own poetry—his sonnet on the silkworm and another on his beloved as she grows old—referring to himself as "our poet" and "the amusing poet,"[43] and he adds several short verse passages that are probably his as well. The poetry is not simply decorative; it also serves to reinforce an argument and often to add a touch of humor through a new image. One example is the scene, expressed in four lines of verse, which compares a lady dressed in brocade and standing on her *pianelle*, or high, wooden platform shoes, to a baldachin, or ceremonial canopy.

Tarabotti was not one to take this criticism of women lightly, even though it was couched in humor. She saw the injustice in reproaching only women for their attention to fashion and not men, whose dress was even more extravagant, and she decried the unequal position of women in society that prevented them from defending themselves since they lacked the education and the opportunity to do so. Unlike most women, Tarabotti had the ability to take on the challenge and she had a public voice: she had just published her *Paradiso monacale* and *Soliloquio*.

Tarabotti states that she responded to Buoninsegni only at the insistence of important women who had brought his satire to her attention, and that she was unhappy they had failed to keep their promise not to publish what she wrote—or,

42. This canto of Ariosto's epic-chivalric poem (1532) presents a novella, the story of Fiammetta and Astolfo, which demonstrates that it is the nature of all women to be unfaithful. Ariosto's ironic opening of the canto suggests that the story it narrates should not be taken seriously but instead given the consideration one would give to "fiction and fable" (gli dia quella medesima credenza / che si suol dare a finzioni e a fole). Ariosto, *Orlando furioso*, ed. Cesare Segre, 5th ed. (Milan: Mondadori, 1990), XXVIII, 3:3–4.

43. "Questo del fasto altrui gravido seme" (This fertile seed of another's pomp) and "Già sovra l'alpi del tuo bianco crine" (Now upon the alpine heights of your white hair). For a critical edition of these and all of Buoninsegni's known sonnets, see Melchor i Fenollosa, "Sonets esparsos."

more precisely, not to let any man see it. The claim that she did not want to publish her response is entirely implausible and must be understood to be a gesture of self-defense, an effort to protect herself from the criticism that such a publication by a nun would certainly provoke. On the *Antisatira* frontispiece Tarabotti seeks to disassociate herself superficially from the publication, permitting only her initials "D. A. T." (Donna Arcangela Tarabotti) and not her full name to appear (fig. 3). Hiding beneath these initials not only concealed her identity as a woman religious but may also have assisted her in securing the necessary publishing privilege. Indeed the publisher, Francesco Valvasense, was complicit in this fiction and claims in his note "To the Readers" that, though he was unable to get Tarabotti's permission, he managed to steal the manuscript from someone who had a copy. Yet it is clear from Tarabotti's letters and corroborated in the *Antisatira* that she was fully behind the publication of her response, as is apparent in the way she addresses her readers. For example, she introduces her portrayal of the fashionable gentleman of her day in the *Antisatira* as follows: "I wish to stage, *before the eyes of the entire world,* men dressed in the current fashion" (86, my emphasis).[44] Her claim is also contradicted in letters where she discusses her efforts to bring the text to press despite the opposition to it by Angelico Aprosio and her brother-in-law Giacomo Pighetti.[45] It would seem to be contradicted as well by her letter to the Grand Duchess of Tuscany Vittoria della Rovere asking permission to dedicate the work to her, and in the dedication itself in which Tarabotti asks the grand duchess to protect her "from the malevolent bite of the snarling critics who attack and wish to wound me."[46]

Tarabotti employs various tactics in her response to Buoninsegni. She is polite and even adulatory when she addresses him directly. She praises his reputation both as a gentleman and as an intellectual, a subtle wit, a writer of admirable

44. "[V]oglio far comparir in iscena agli occhi di tutto il mondo gli uomini vestiti all'uso moderno." Tarabotti, *Antisatira* (Weaver), 97.

45. To Pighetti: "It was not ambition that persuaded me to publish this little work of mine." Tarabotti, *Letters*, 165–66 (letter 113). To Aprosio: "since your Lordship is partial to Buoninsegni, you would like me to refrain from speaking of him, and therefore you try to dissuade me by labeling this truth which is so pleasing to God as a satire and an improper battle for a woman religious. But be this as it may, I persevere in my righteous opinions, and therefore I will not yield from this one" (Essendo Vostra Signoria parziale del Buoninsegni, mi vorrebbe senza lingua per lui, e perciò va dissuadendomi col dar titolo di satire e duelli impropri ad una buona religiosa alla verità tanto grata a Dio. Ma siassi come si voglia, io sono perseverante nelle mie buone opinioni, perciò non mi rimovo da questa). Tarabotti, *Letters*, 173–74 (letter 122); Tarabotti, *Lettere*, 181.

46. From the dedication, Tarabotti, *Antisatire*, 32: "A voi però ricorro, semidea della Toscana, … perché mi siate scudo contro ai colpi delle maligne dentature de' mordaci." Tarabotti, *Antisatira* (Weaver), 32. In her letter to Vittoria della Rovere, she writes: "I have resolved that the printed work will seek protection beneath the wing of that same deity to whom I dedicated the manuscript" (ho rissoluto che sotto alla protezione di quel nume a cui la consacrai manuscritta, ella ricorrà per patrocinio anche stampata). Tarabotti, *Letters*, 89–90 (letter 33); Tarabotti, *Lettere*, 90.

eloquence, a prudent, modest man, and more, but she is unrelenting in her criticism of his discourse and of the attitudes he expresses regarding women. For this, she says, he is an indefensible enemy of women, and for having accepted the task of delivering the discourse—even if unwillingly, as he claims—he is an individual of too little conviction. She is polite but not convincing when she reminds herself and her reader again and again that Buoninsegni purports to speak only in jest. If she seems to accept his excuses, she is adamant about the consequences his accusations—even if made in jest—have on the lives and good reputation of women; and she returns throughout her work to the effects that misogynist literature and the societal norms it promotes have had on her life. This issue gives rise to several vehement polemical digressions in her response. Buoninsegni makes a reference to Cato that provokes the following protest against the practice of the enforced monachization of women:

> You have different ends in mind when you detest the extravagances of women. He [Cato] desired to see the freedom of the Roman people conserved, and you undermine the freedom of women. That great father of the country would not view without disdain the tyranny used today to imprison women.[47] (80)

With a leap of logic, Tarabotti argues that their combination of beauty and piety associates women with the divine, and that their actions are exemplary. Therefore, she concludes, women should be beautifully adorned, honored, and revered—yet the response of men is instead to malign and exclude them:

> today, poor feminine justice and sanctity, or rather, poor women, for all your justice and sanctity you are excluded from every position of honor, from every function in public forums. Ever more greatly maligned, we are held as prisoners, because every day the perfidy of men grows greater.[48] (63)

By switching from the "you" with which she addresses women at the beginning of this passage to the inclusive "we are held prisoners," Tarabotti adds the injustice done to her personally to the general case. She has been confined in a convent against her will, denied an education, and thereby excluded from

47. "E voi con fini diversi da lui detestate le pompe feminili. Egli bramava di veder conservato libero il popolo di Roma, e voi sète insidiatori della libertà donnesca." Tarabotti, *Antisatira* (Weaver), 89. Buoninsegni refers to Cato the Censor; Tarabotti makes it a reference to Cato Uticensis. See Tarabotti, *Antisatire*, 80, and note 72.

48. "Ma oggidì, povera giustizia e santità feminile, anzi povere donne, poiché con tutta la vostra giustizia e santità sète escluse da ogni dignità, da ogni fonzione de' fori e ogn'ora piú vilipese siam tenute prigioniere, perch'ogni giorno più cresce la perfidia negli uomini." Tarabotti, *Antisatira* (Weaver), 67.

public life. As she puts it in her *Semplicità ingannata* (*Paternal Tyranny*), by being considered inferior and subordinated to men, women are deprived of free will. Unable to find support as yet in Italy to publish the polemical treatise in which she has laid out her thoughts systematically, Tarabotti finds a way to do so sporadically in her response to Buoninsegni's attack.

In the *Antisatira*, Tarabotti also answers the "malevolent" and "snarling critics" mentioned in the dedication, who claim she could not be the author of *Paradiso monacale*:[49] "Let these great literati croak as much as they like, ... but let them also know that I take no greater pride in any other merit of my book than that no men have had a hand in it" (69).[50] If her critics "croak," she speaks with the voice of a "raucous cicada" (69)—that is, with a sharp, unrelenting feminine voice that can hold its own with theirs.[51]

Tarabotti has a long view. Misogyny is as old as Adam. "The first words that came out of the mouth of the first man," she writes, "were in accusation of a woman. From this event I deduce what one can expect from other men."[52] She further notes, sarcastically:

> What a marvel it is that we hear nothing but the denigration of women, on the authority of philosophers, jurists, orators, and poets, and even through purposeful misreadings of Holy Scripture, if almost all those who write and have written are men![53] (77)

It is difficult, despite her frequent disclaimers, to separate Buoninsegni—whom she calls "the most gentlemanly satirist" (66)[54]—and the attitudes he expresses in his discourse from those she attributes to all men. She calls men

49. "And so it has happened that many evil tongues and ignorant men claim that *Convent Paradise* cannot be the product of my wits or the flight of my pen, or else, if it were so, it must necessarily have been embellished, ornamented, and enriched with elements of philosophy and theology borrowed from men of superior intelligence" (Percio è avvenuto che molti maligni o ignoranti asseriscano che 'l *Paradiso monacale* non possa esser dettame dell'ingegno mio, o volo della mia penna, o pur, che, essendo, sia anche necessità ch'abbia ricevuto ornamento, fregi, e ricchezze di tratti di filosofia e teologia da spiriti elevati e intelligenti). Tarabotti, *Antisatire*, 68; Tarabotti, *Antisatira* (Weaver), 74.

50. "Gracchino pur a lor voglia questi gran letterati, ma però sappiano ch'io non mi glorio d'altra buona qualità di questo mio libro se non solo ch'uomini non gli abbiano posto dentro mano." Tarabotti, *Antisatira* (Weaver), 74.

51. "strepitosa cicala." Tarabotti, *Antisatira* (Weaver), 75.

52. From "To the Reader" in Tarabotti, *Antisatire*, 56–57: "[Le] prime parole ch'uscirono dalla bocca al primo di loro, benché poc'anzi fosse stato creato dalla mano di Dio, furono in accusa della donna. Da questo successo, argomento ciò che si possa credere degli altri." Tarabotti, *Antisatira* (Weaver), 58.

53. "Qual maraviglia è che non si senta altro che sparlar delle donne con auttorità di filosofi, di leggisti, d'oratori, e poeti, e sino con stiracchiamenti della Sacra Scrittura, se quasi tutti coloro che scrivono e hanno scritto son uomini." Tarabotti, *Antisatira* (Weaver), 84.

54. "Il nostro gentilissimo satirico." Tarabotti, *Antisatira* (Weaver), 70.

evil, tyrannical, and cruel; and in their dress vain, effete, and worthless, only occasionally, in an aside, remembering to exempt Buoninsegni from this company. While there is no reason to think that she harbors any personal animus toward Buoninsegni, it is very likely that her deference to him in the *Antisatira* was strengthened in the text at the urging of Pighetti, who advised her to do so after he had read the draft she sent him. She says as much in a letter she wrote him to complain that once the *Antisatira* was published he turned against her:[55]

> If your Eminent Lordship could recall the sentiments you expressed to me when first I showed you my *Antisatire*, you would not now behave in this way, for you never told me I should not publish it, but only suggested, I recall, that I take out a number of words that seemed to you too biased against Signor Buoninsegni, which I promptly did. Since I still have the manuscript, I can show you.[56]

Despite her rebuttal of much of what Buoninsegni has to say, Tarabotti occasionally agrees with her adversary. She admits that women should not dedicate themselves excessively to expensive clothes and jewelry, but she points out that men do so as well and are even guiltier, yet they are not called out for it. She dismisses other criticisms and insists on the virtues of women, accusing men of mistreating them and of denying them their due while spending their dowries on illicit loves. She insists that women have a right to cultivate and enhance their beauty with art, that they were created superior to men, and that this is justly expressed by their long and elegant dresses and the high shoes that serve as a pedestal on which to revere them.

Tarabotti has an answer for each of Buoninsegni's accusations but not always following his order, often abandoning it to engage in serious critique. In both the *Satira* and the *Antisatira*, digression is the rule, not the exception. Buoninsegni includes anecdotes that showcase his classical learning; Tarabotti finds a place for the polemics that characterize all her writing. Both antagonists appeal to authorities, ancient and modern, but Tarabotti strengthens her arguments by calling on

55. Pighetti supposedly encouraged Aprosio to respond in writing to the *Antisatira*, which he did with great vehemence and insult in a work he entitled *La Maschera scoperta* (The mask lifted). Aprosio gives his account in Angelico Aprosio, *La biblioteca aprosiana, passatempo autunnale di Cornelio Apasio Antivigilmi* [pseud.] (Bologna: Per li Manolessi, 1673), 167–68. See the discussion below (pages 23–27) on responses to the *Antisatira*.

56. Tarabotti, *Letters*, 165 (letter 113). "Se Vostra Signoria Clarissima si riducesse a memoria i sensi ch'Ella m'espose quando già tempo le feci vedere la mia *Antisatira*, non trattarebbe ora in modo tale, perché Ella non mai mi disse che non dovessi darla in luce, ma solo, mi raccordo, il cancellarle molte parole ch'a Lei parevano in pregiudicio del signor Boninsegni, il che essequii con ogni pontualità e, avendola pur ancora manuscritta, potrò fargliele vedere." Tarabotti, *Lettere*, 172 (letter 113).

divine authority and by defending her positions with passages from the Bible and from liturgy.

Tarabotti takes up the bizarre analogies proposed by Buoninsegni and either seeks to outdo him in rhetorical competition or declares them to be illogical and unworthy of such a distinguished writer. Missing in her response is her usual heavy use of elaborate and entertaining conceits of her own; they are not entirely absent, but rarer than a reader of her other works would expect. For the most part she simply builds upon those in Buoninsegni's satire, either taking issue with them or developing them differently—as she does, for instance, with his use of playing card suits to exemplify women's behavior.

It is only toward the end of the *Antisatira*, where Tarabotti departs from Buoninsegni's text to denounce the vanities of men, that her usual, imaginative prose appears in a long and sustained burlesque comparison of men's dress with that of children. She claims that even as men grow older they enjoy "frivolities and childish things" (*fanciullagini e frascherie*); "they behave like children and become childlike" (*bamboleggiano e rimbambiscono nell'intelletto*); they "dress like juveniles" (*vestono … di puerili arnesi il corpo*); and "their minds are immature" (*siano … tanti fanciulli d'ingegno*) (87). This opening is followed by a long list of articles of male dress that are strikingly similar to the clothes of infants and nursing babies—their lace bibs, for example, their suspenders and sashes, the swathes of cloth they wrap around themselves (they "putteggiano"; they are like "bambini," "piccioli bambollini" and a "puttino lattante").[57]

In his satire, Buoninsegni paints a portrait of the fashion-conscious lady at her toilette as her housemaid constructs an enormous hairdo with hemp cords, staves, ribbons, and pearls. The lady may also wear an expensive wig and when it is time will dye her hair. She is dressed in the finest long silk gowns, is bedecked with jewels, and is perched on tall gilded or silver platform shoes. This portrait of a lady is drawn with broad strokes, but Tarabotti concludes her response by putting on stage, as she says, for the world to see, a meticulous head to toe depiction of the stylish contemporary gentleman—the *précieux* or dandy of the time whom Buoninsegni has left out of his diatribe against the vanities. Tarabotti corrects the injustice of Buoninsegni's critique by providing the missing counterpart as irrefutable evidence that, if women err, men do so to an even greater degree.

Tarabotti's description is a tour de force—an example of her prose at its most entertaining. She begins with his hair, so long and full that he wears out a dozen combs on it and as many hot irons on his curls, beard, and moustache. Moustaches seem to have amused Tarabotti more than any other male fashion

57. Tarabotti, *Antisatira* (Weaver), 100. Unfortunately, English lacks the vast Italian system of noun and verb endings that would make it possible to do justice in translation to the variety in Tarabotti's extended etymological figures.

statement (she ridicules them also in *Paternal Tyranny*).[58] This is the second time she mentions them in her response and she is brief here, since she has already written that men "have so altered the natural shape of their moustaches that instead of falling over their lips to obstruct their obscene masculine speech they are constrained by iron and fire to raise themselves up menacingly toward the sky" (84).[59] Her gentleman's garments are made of sumptuous silks, velvets, and damasks that are heavily decorated with the finest lace; his linen shirt, revealed through well-placed cuts in his coat, is embellished with embroidery and raised-needle lace. She proceeds in this manner, listing all the baubles on his coat and cuffs, his heavy jewelry, his English hose—each item described in great detail down to his shoes, whose inordinate heels cause him to walk awkwardly as though he were a shod horse. To add to the humor at her gentleman's expense she notes that the toes of his hose and shoes are crescent-shaped so that his feet will not envy the "insignia of Diana" that many men wear on their heads.[60]

In her message "To the Reader" that precedes her response to Buoninsegni, Tarabotti insists that she has not written "a *Vanities of Men* [*Lusso virile*], or a *Countersatire* [*Contrasatira*], out of spiteful vendetta," but adds that should Buoninsegni "feel he has been stung ... he should not take offense, since the provocation comes from him" (56).[61] Yet in the *Antisatira* itself, just after her complaint that men do not believe a woman could write with good style and wit, she cites lines from a sonnet by Cesare Orsini entitled "Huomo malvagio" (Evil Man) that she has altered so that they promise vendetta at the hands of a woman for the evils of men: she concludes in the first person threatening "with my words I will take up the sword / and press and wound with invincible force" (79). At the end of

58. Tarabotti, *Paternal Tyranny*, 133. On mustaches, hair, wigs, and in general men's and women's styles as well as their social significance, see Eugenia Paulicelli, "Sister Arcangela Tarabotti: Hair, Wigs and Other Vices," in Paulicelli, *Writing Fashion in Early Modern Italy: From "Sprezzatura" to Satire* (Aldershot, Farnham, Surrey, UK: Ashgate, 2014), 177–204, esp. 186–201.

59. "Hanno alterato sin il moto naturale ai mostachi, che, invece di cader pendenti sopra il labro ad impedir l'uscita all'oscenità delle parole virili, son forzati dal ferro e dal fuoco ad inalzasi minancianti verso il cielo." Tarabotti, *Antisatira* (Weaver), 96.

60. The *Satire* and *Antisatire* are valuable documents for the history of fashion. The costume historian Rita Levi-Pisetzky refers frequently in her studies to the *Antisatira* for descriptions of seventeenth-century Italian male attire. See Rita Levi-Pisetzky, "Il gusto barocco nel costume italiano del Seicento," *Studi secenteschi* 2 (1961): 61–94; Rita Levi-Pisetzky, *Storia del costume in Italia*, vol. 3, *Il Seicento* (Rome: Istituto Editoriale Italiano, 1966), 301–481; and Rita Levi-Pisetzky, *Il costume e la moda nella società italiana* (Turin: Einaudi, 1978). Tarabotti refers here to the "insegna di Diana"—that is, the crescent moon that appears with upturned points on the head of the goddess Diana as she is often represented. On a man's head they would seem horns and, Tarabotti suggests, would indicate that he is a cuckold.

61. "M'acerto che alcuni uomini non potranno, se non mendacemente, dire ch'io formi un *Lusso virile*, o una *Contrasatira*, per isdegnosa vendetta .... Se 'l signor Buoninsegni si sentirà pungere, essendo gentiluomo prudentissimo, non dovrebbe sdegnarsene, sapendo che 'l motivo viene da lui." Tarabotti, *Antisatira* (Weaver), 56–57.

the *Antisatira* Tarabotti claims that her adversary has in common with Orpheus both the sweetness of his song and his abhorrence of women, and she suggests that the vendetta of the Maenads was perhaps merited, implying that Buoninsegni too will have deserved the "sting" he has received at her hand.

The *Antisatira* is the first of two works that Tarabotti subtitled *Difesa della donna* (Defense of Women) and clearly, though in a somewhat indirect way, she claims that through these works she vindicates womankind and strikes a blow against their detractors.[62] Filled with such detail and so many digressions, the *Antisatira* far exceeds the length of Buoninsegni's *Satira*.[63]

Tarabotti had initially thought she would dedicate the *Antisatira* to Leopoldo de' Medici, but instead she turned to his sister-in-law Vittoria della Rovere, Grand Duchess of Tuscany, wife of Grand Duke Ferdinando II de' Medici (fig. 4), hoping in this way to garner favor and perhaps enlist the grand duchess's help in publishing *Tirannia paterna* (*Paternal Tyranny*). Vittoria della Rovere was known to support women artists, singers, and musicians; she and the other Medici women were active in their support of female convents.[64] Moreover, as the grand duchess was a strong and well-educated woman, Tarabotti could expect that she would favor a work that defended women—and, in the case of the *Antisatira*, the elegant dress required of a woman of the grand duchess's class and position. Indeed it is known that Vittoria frequently inquired about the latest French fashions.[65] Tarabotti wrote to the grand duchess on July 9, 1644, to ask permission to dedicate the *Antisatira* to

62. The other work is *Women Are of the Human Species: Defense of Women by Galerana Barcitotti* [pseud.]. See 10–11, and note 31.

63. A reference to the greater length of Tarabotti's response appears in the preface to Sesti, *Censura*, 110: "Se il ragionare e la ragione fossero l'istesso (oh signora Angelica [*sic*]) crederei al certo che voi tanta piú ragione havessi del signor Buoninsegni quanto piú di lui havete ragionato" (If reasoning [talking] and reason were the same thing (oh signora Angelica [*sic*]), I would certainly believe that you had greater reason [were more to believe] than signor Buoninsegni, since your reasoning went on longer).

64. On Vittoria della Rovere in general and specifically on her patronage of women in the arts, see Eve Straussman-Pflanzer, "Court Culture in Seventeenth-Century Florence: The Art Patronage of Medici Grand Duchess Vittoria della Rovere (1622–1694)" (PhD diss., New York University Institute of Fine Arts, 2010) and Giovanna Benadusi, "The Gender Politics of Vittoria della Rovere," in *Medici Women: The Making of a Dynasty in Grand Ducal Tuscany*, ed. Giovanna Benadusi and Judith C. Brown (Toronto: Centre for Reformation and Renaissance Studies, 2015), 264–301. These and other recent studies have painted a multifaceted picture of the grand duchess, who has been portrayed simply as "bigoted" by historians, mostly male, who have not studied her and who have attributed to her religious fervor the ineffective rule of her son Cosimo III. For the complex role she played in supporting women in matrimonial disputes and inheritance issues, in assisting orphans and widows, and generally in her vast correspondence with women, see Giovanna Benadusi, "Carteggi e negozi della granduchessa Vittoria della Rovere, 1634–1694," in *Le donne Medici nel sistema europeo delle corti, XVI–XVII secolo: Atti del convegno internazionale, Firenze, San Domenico di Fiesole, 6–8 ottobre 2005*, ed. Giulia Calvi and Riccardo Spinelli (Florence: Polistampa, 2008), 1:415–31.

65. Benadusi, "Carteggi," 421.

her and nine days later she received a positive response in which the grand duchess wrote: "I am happy knowing that your study and your attention to a subject that truly requires a reply will be rewarded with deserved praise."[66] The grand duchess may not have yet read the *Antisatira* when she wrote but she knew from Tarabotti's letter and very likely from the dedicatory letter that would appear in the publication that her work was a defense of women's fashions. Encouraged by the grand duchess's positive response, Tarabotti again wrote to her on April 8, 1645, expressing gratitude for her extraordinary kindness and requesting her assistance in publishing *Tirannia paterna*: "I dare beg you to lend me the support of your most authoritative patronage in order to obtain from Rome, or else from Florence, the publishing privileges to have my *Tirannia paterna* printed, which for certain reasons I do not seek in my own state."[67] It seems the response to this request was silence. The two other letters Tarabotti wrote to the grand duchess in that year, the last of their correspondence, merely conveyed good wishes, and the response she received was a very brief expression of thanks and a request to remain in her prayers. If the grand duchess read the *Antisatira*—and even if not, given the title itself of *Tirannia paterna*—this would have sufficed to dissuade her from offering assistance.

The Reception

Before publishing her work, Tarabotti sent it to two men on whom she thought she could rely for good advice and support: her friend and correspondent Angelico Aprosio and her brother-in-law Giacomo Pighetti. Both men responded negatively. Aprosio urged her not to publish it, declaring it "full of absurdities and … impertinences."[68] Pighetti found some of her references to Buoninsegni offensive. Francesco Buoninsegni, however, when it was brought to his attention that Tarabotti had written a response to his discourse, wrote to Aprosio:

> I am infinitely grateful to that reverend mother who has honored me by finding my bagatelles, written to entertain our Most Serene Patron for an hour at the Academy, worthy of the censure of her exalted wit.[69]

66. "Mi rallegro che riporterà quella lode che merita il Suo studio et la Sua applicazione ad un concetto che veram[ent]e ammette replica." Medioli, "Arcangela Tarabotti's Reliability," 86. On the exchange of letters between Tarabotti and Vittoria della Rovere as well as an edition of the texts, see Medioli, "Arcangela Tarabotti's Reliability," 81–91.

67. Tarabotti, *Letters*, 147 (letter 94): "Oso di supplicarLa a porgermi il braccio del Suo autorevolissimo patrocinio ad ottener di Roma, over da Firenze, le licenze di dar alle stampe la mia *Tirania paterna* che per certi miei fini non ricerco nella mia patria." Tarabotti, *Lettere*, 152.

68. Aprosio, *La biblioteca aprosiana*, 168: "ripiena di mille spropositi e di non poche impertinenze."

69. Letter to Aprosio, dated September 15, 1644, Genoa, Biblioteca Universitaria (BUG), E VI 6, cited in a chapter on Tarabotti in Portigliotti, *Penombre*, 285: "Io rendo infinite gratie a quella madre, che

When he received a copy, he wrote again to Aprosio:

> I received the nun's book and, immediately with four gentlemen of the Academy who were present when I received it, I read it straight through and to the supreme pleasure of everyone. We marveled at the great intelligence of that reverend mother. If Your Reverence has occasion to speak to her, I ask you to give her a most affectionate kiss on the hand for me, thanking her with all my heart for the honor she has given me with her most erudite response. Assure her that not only have I not taken badly her little stings but I have been extremely grateful for them, and if I ever come to Venice, as I hope to soon, I will attest my gratitude to her in person. For now give her my warm greetings.[70]

A few years later, in 1650, Buoninsegni paid homage again to Tarabotti when he read his satire *Delle sciocchezze degli huomini* (The foolishness of men) to the Academy of the Filomati. In this satire he represents himself humorously as one who has suffered at the hands of women because of his criticism eighteen years earlier of their fashions. He claims that he has been the object of their scorn and has been hit by thousands of ladies' shoes, but that should now be enough, since the vendetta of one of them has punished him sufficiently for them all.

Even though my flesh and bones are broken	*Sebbene ho già le carni e l'ossa strutte*
I no longer need repent nor to the priest pay	*E per la penetenza andar dal Prete*
Visit. Your complaints now please forestall,	*Hor non occorre più: state pur chete*
One woman has waged vendetta for you all.	*Che fatte ha le vendette una per tutte.*[71]

In general the reaction to Tarabotti's intervention in the debate was astonishment: some admired her courage and others objected to the effrontery of a nun who would challenge a well-known and respected man of letters in the

---

ha voluto honorarmi, stimando le mie bagatelle fatte per far ridere un'hora nell'Accademia degne delle censure dell'ingegno elevato di cotesta madre."

70. Letter to Aprosio, dated Siena, December 21, 1644, Genoa, BUG, E VI 6, and Portigliotti, *Penombre claustrali*, 285: "ricevei il libro della Monaca, e subito con i Gentilhuomini Accad.ci che erano presenti, quando lo ricevei, lo lessi in un fiato con sommo piacere di tutti, che restammo maravigliati del grand'ingegno di cotesta Madre; alla quale se V. P. ha occasione di parlare, desidero che faccia da mia parte un affettuosissimo baciamani, ringraziadola con tutto l'animo dell'honore che mi ha fatto con la sua eruditissima risposta, assicurandola che non solo non ho avute per male le punture che ella mi dà, ma da me sono state gradite in estremo, e se mai verrò a Venetia, come spero in breve, a bocca le ne attesterò la mia gratitudine."

71. Buoninsegni, *Delle sciocchezze degli huomini*. Florence, BNCF, Magliabechi VII 456, fol. 57v (stanza 22).

service of the Medici. Tarabotti lamented all the outcry in favor of Buoninsegni, which she declared to be unnecessary and inappropriate.[72] Several writers, some erstwhile friends among them, penned responses to the *Antisatira*.[73] Aprosio wrote a polemical and mean-spirited response entitled *La Maschera scoperta* (The mask lifted) whose publication, however, Tarabotti was able to suppress through the intervention of powerful friends.[74] In his commentary Aprosio objects point by point to the *Antisatira*, citing authorities at length, many very obscure, in a pompous show of tedious erudition. He refers to Tarabotti with condescension throughout, and often with insults.[75] He also makes insinuations about her morality and vanity.[76] He ends the tract inferring that she should return "to the labors of Arachne, to the needle and the spindle" (Ai lavori d'Aracne, a l'ago ai fusi).[77] What clearly aroused her ire, however—far more than his disagreements with her response to Buoninsegni and his arrogance—was surely the long passage in which he insists that she could not have written *Paradiso monacale* without help, and that perhaps even *Tirannia paterna* was the work of more than one hand.[78] Later, in 1646, Aprosio succeeded in publishing a different and much revised response, *Lo Scudo di Rinaldo, overo Lo specchio del disinganno* (The shield of Rinaldo, or The mirror of disillusion), in which he opposed the ideas expressed in the *Antisatira* but without the *ad personam* attacks on Tarabotti of his earlier attempt.[79] In the *Scudo*, he mentions her openly only in a list of noteworthy women of letters, but he does not fail to include an insult, writing "I think it is worse to have a wife who is crippled than one who is cross-eyed or hunchback," an obvious allusion to Tarabotti's limp.[80]

72. See Tarabotti, *Letters*, 164–66 (letter 113).

73. For a history of the responses to the *Antisatire*, and especially those of Aprosio, see Biga, *Una polemica antifemminista.*

74. *"La maschera scoperta" di Filofilo Misoponero* [pseud.] *in risposta all'"Antisatira" di D. A. T. scritta contro la "Satira menippea" del signor Francesco Buoninsegni*, in Biga, *Una polemica antifemminista*, 93–174. See Aprosio, *La biblioteca aprosiana*, 168–69, and Biga, *Una polemica antifemminista*, 63.

75. For example, he refers to her as "Signora Smascherata" (Unmasked Lady), "Signora Apologista" (Lady Apologist), "Signora Avversaria" (Lady Adversary), "Signora Ponerofila" (Evil-loving Lady), "Signora Filaula," (Lady Court-lover), "Signora Filocosma" (Lady Lover of Cosmetics), "Signora Filasotìa," (Lady Lover of Dissipation), "Signora A[rcangela]," "Signora T[arabotti]," etc. On Aprosio's response, see Marini, "Angelico Aprosio da Ventimiglia," 171–72.

76. Biga, *Una polemica antifemminista*, 115, 126, 159.

77. Biga, *Una polemica antifemminista*, 172. See also Paulicelli, "Sister Arcangela," 196–98.

78. Biga, *Una polemica antifemminista*, 140.

79. Angelico Aprosio, *Lo Scudo di Rinaldo, overo Lo specchio del disinganno, opera di Scipio Glareano* [pseud.] (Venice: Gio. Iacomo Hertz, 1646).

80. "Credo però esser peggio aver in moglie una zoppa che una guercia o pura una gobba." Aprosio, *Lo Scudo*, 295, cited in Biga, *Una polemica antifemminista*, 71. The passage in the *Scudo* in which Tarabotti is listed among women of letters deserving of praise is cited in Portigliotti, *Penombre claustrali*, 294.

Both Tarabotti and Buoninsegni refer to Brusoni's *Antisatira satirizzata* (Antisatire satirized) in their letters: Buoninsegni in two letters written to Aprosio, one in which he asks him to procure a copy for him from the author;[81] Tarabotti, writing to her friend Nicolas Bretel de Grémonville, the French ambassador to Venice. Bretel had asked about the polemics engendered by the *Antisatira*, and Tarabotti responded:

> Thus far the *Antisatire satirized*, which is the best, has not been put to press. *The mask lifted* has not been seen and quite likely they both could have been reduced to ashes in the *Funeral for feminine luxury* that came out from Bologna.[82]

Tarabotti seems to have read Brusoni's *Antisatira satirizzata* in manuscript. The Funeral for feminine luxury (*Funerale delle pompe feminili*) is also mentioned by Aprosio in *La Maschera scoperta* where he attributes it to a Silvio Foccacci and claims it was about to appear in Orvieto.[83] No known copy of either of these responses has survived.

In 1656, four years after Tarabotti's death, Ludovico Sesti, a Dominican friar and academy member from Lucca, published the *Censura dell'Antisatira* (Censure of the Antisatire) using the pseudonym Lucido Ossiteo.[84] The *Censura* was published in Siena together with the *Satira* and *Antisatira*. Tarabotti might have read it in manuscript, but there is no mention of it in any of her works. While less offensive and less tedious than Aprosio's *La Maschera scoperta*, the *Censura* shares its misogyny and its condescension. Sesti calls Tarabotti a woman of only a little learning—literally "with a dusting of only a few words" (una femmina infarinata di quattro vocaboli) and he admonishes her for daring to challenge a member of

81. Biga, *Una polemica antifemminista*, 84; see also Buoninsegni's letters to Aprosio, Genoa, BUG, Mss. E VI 6.

82. Tarabotti, *Letters*, 151–52 (letter 99): "Sinora l'*Antisatira satirizzata*, che è la migliore, non è uscita alla luce. La *Maschera discoperta* non s'è veduta e facilmente potrebbero essersi ambedue incenerite nei *Funerali delle pompe feminili* che venivano di Bologna." Tarabotti, *Lettere*, 157. Immediately following the quoted passage, Tarabotti also threatens her own responses: to the *Antisatira satirizzata* (Antisatire satirized), an *Ercole geromicida* (Hercules Slayer of Geryon), which would hit it "with bolts of lightning," and to *La Maschera scoperta* (The mask lifted), a comedy entitled *Ardire* (Boldness) to ridicule Aprosio, whom she calls the "puppet" who wrote it. Neither of these works, if actually written, has survived.

83. See the edition of the revised manuscript of *La maschera scoperta*, dated 1671 and published in Biga, *Una polemica antifemminista*, 140. This work and the author Silvio Foccacci are also mentioned in Zanette, *Suor Arcangela*, 278, but neither Biga nor Zanette identify this author nor have I found any other information about him.

84. Sesti, *Censura*.

the Sienese academy and Italy's premier intellectual.[85] Sesti ridicules Tarabotti's desire for an education, saying that she is no more cut out for study than Hercules is for spinning.[86] Yet he also expresses regard for her reputation as a writer even while disparaging her advocacy of learning for women—issues that recur in the *Censura* more frequently than in *La Maschera scoperta*.

In the years immediately following this exchange, writers generally associated with the academies of Italy continued to ridicule the extravagant fashions of the time, and, in keeping with their misogyny, especially—but not exclusively—those of women. They took aim as well at the effeminacy and excessive ornamentation of men's attire, in verse and in prose. Agostino Lampugnani, another member of the Incogniti, published in 1648 a humorous discourse on the excesses of men's and women's fashions, the *Carrozza da nolo, overo Del vestire e usanze alla moda* (Rented carriage, or Of fashionable clothing and customs), with successive editions in 1649 and 1655.[87] Some of the interest was clearly created by the literary debate that centered on the *Antisatira* and the responses it engendered, but the topic was not new in the seventeenth century. The costume historian Rita Levi-Pisetzky finds examples of the condemnation of wasteful and deceptive dress in Italian literature as early as the thirteenth century in Jacopone da Todi's *Satira XVII* and in the sermons of preachers, the most eloquent of whom was San Bernardino of Siena (1380–1444).[88] The renewed interest in the subject was a product of academy culture and a response to the excesses—but also the entertaining indulgences—of Baroque taste.

While Tarabotti had hoped her real success would come with the publication of her life's work, *Tirannia paterna*, she first reached an audience beyond the

85. "E chi siete voi che ardimentosa vi cimentate col primo ingegno d'Italia? Sareste mai piú che una femmina infarinata di quatro vocaboli? E vi ponete a petto per rispondere ad un huomo accademico sanese?" Sesti, *Censura*, 110.

86. "E perché non studiate? Chi vi tiene? Confessatela giusta, non è arte vostra. Non vi s'avviene piú che ad Ercole il filare. La sella disdice al somaro. La scimmia è sempre scimmia" (And why don't you study? Who is holding you back? Tell it truthfully: it is not an art for you. It is no more appropriate for you than spinning for Hercules. A saddle is not for a donkey. A monkey is always a monkey). Sesti, *Censura*, 128.

87. Agostino Lampugnani, *Carrozza da nolo, overo Del vestire e usanze alla moda di Gio. Sonta Pagnalmino* [pseud.] (Bologna: Carlo Zenero, 1648). It appeared again in 1649 (Milan: Lodovico Monza) and in 1655 (Venice: Giacomo Bortoli). On Lampugnani, see Levi-Pisetzky, *Il costume e la moda*, 241–44, and Paulicelli, "*La moda* and Its Technologies: Agostino Lampugnani's 'La carrozza da nolo, ovvero Del vestire e usanze alla moda': The Rented Carriage, or Of Clothing and Fashionable Habits [*sic*], 1648–1650," in Paulicelli, *Writing Fashion*, 205–23. See also a satire of fashion in seventeenth-century Naples written by Andrea Genuzio, *Satira ed Antisatira*, ed. Girolamo de Miranda (Rome: Salerno Editrice, 1997), which originally appeared in 1640 with the full title *Satira ed Antisatira contro gli abbigliamenti degli uomini e delle donne* (Satire and Antisatire against the dress of men and women).

88. Levi-Pisetzky, *Il costume e la moda*, 17–18.

convent with the publication of the *Soliloquio* and *Paradiso monacale.* With the publication of the *Antisatira* she found a place for herself in the literary world, and it was primarily with this work that she first became a known personality, a public figure, in Venice and beyond.

Note on the Text and Translation

Arcangela Tarabotti published two editions of the combined *Satira* of Francesco Buoninsegni and her *Antisatira* in response to Buoninsegni. Her second edition includes many corrections that she requested and should be considered her authorized version of her work. I have based my translation of both works on this edition. See my discussion and analysis of the differences between these two 1644 editions in Francesco Buoninsegni and Arcangela Tarabotti, *Satira e Antisatira*, 109–16. I refer to the first Venetian edition as 1644 V1 and to the second as 1644 V2.

A list of all of the editions of Francesco Buoninsegni's *Contro 'l lusso donnesco, Satira menippea* and Tarabotti's *Antisatira* is included in the Bibliography.

In my Introduction I quote in English from the present translation of the *Satire* and *Antisatire*. For the Italian I cite from my 1998 edition. For Tarabotti's *Letters*, I use the Italian edition edited by Meredith K. Ray and Lynn Lara Westwater as well as their English translation. For *Paternal Tyranny*, I cite from Letizia Panizza's English translation and for the original Italian I cite from the *Semplicità ingannata* edited by Simona Bortot. Complete references to these editions appear in the Bibliography. For all other texts I cite from the original and from a reliable translation where available. All other translations, unless otherwise indicated, are mine.

In my translation of the *Satira* and *Antisatira* I have attempted to reproduce in English not only the authors' message but also in as much as possible characteristics of the authors' style—especially their use of figurative language and the rhythms of their prose and verse. This has not always been possible, especially in the case of puns that could not be duplicated in English and, in general, in the case of poetry. I have had to break up Tarabotti's long sentences, so characteristic of her syntax, into shorter ones, and I have often had to reorganize the syntax in order to make the message intelligible in English.

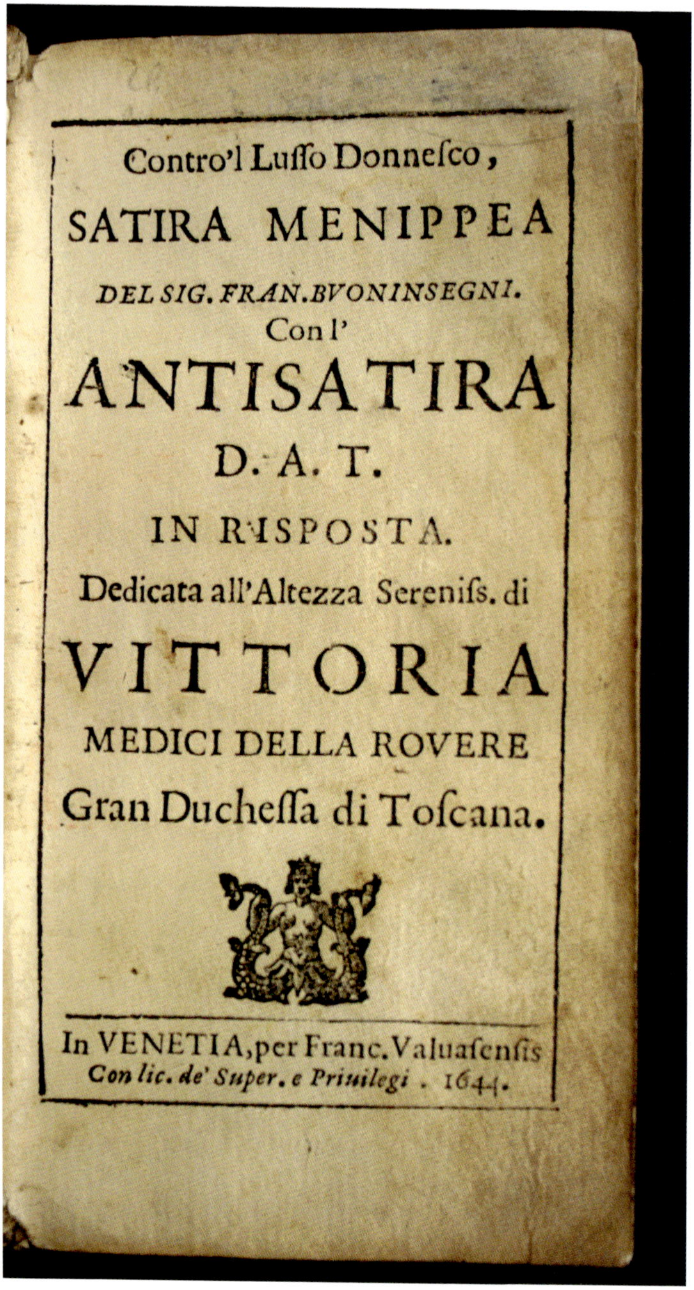
Contro'l Luſſo Donneſco,
SATIRA MENIPPEA
DEL SIG. FRAN. BVONINSEGNI.
Con l'
ANTISATIRA
D. A. T.
IN RISPOSTA.
Dedicata all'Altezza Sereniſs. di
VITTORIA
MEDICI DELLA ROVERE
Gran Ducheſſa di Toſcana.

In VENETIA, per Franc. Valuaſenſis
Con lic. de' Super. e Priuilegi . 1644.

Figure 3. Frontispiece of the *Satira* and *Antisatira* (Venice: 1644). Courtesy of the University of Chicago Library.

Against the Vanities of Women
A MENIPPEAN SATIRE
by Sig. Francesco Buoninsegni
with the
ANTISATIRE
by D[onna] A[rcangela] T[arabotti][1]
in response.
Dedicated to the Most Serene Highness
VITTORIA MEDICI DELLA ROVERE
Grand Duchess of Tuscany[2]

1 Here and elsewhere in the prefatory material Arcangela Tarabotti is referred to by her initials, a pretense that her identity was in this way concealed, since she claims that she did not want it published but it was done without her consent. Yet in a letter she writes "If I did not clearly display my name in the *Antisatire*, it was out of a certain modesty, and not to correct that which I do not regret having done." *Letters*, 280 (letter 252).

2. Vittoria della Rovere (1622–1694) , wife of Grand Duke Ferdinando II de' Medici. See Introduction, 22–23, and note 64.

Dedicatory Letter to the Grand Duchess of Tuscany

Your Most Serene Highness,

Since it is the abusive yet intended purpose of most men in all of their words and actions to hold in contempt and to denigrate women, even though they owe them their birth and their life, Your Most Serene Highness, glory of the female sex in whom celestial qualities abide, and whom I entreat most respectfully, will not disdain to defend your sex. I am persuaded that you will do so out of kindness. Nor do I believe you will belittle this humble gift, which to gain glory for myself I place on the altar of these pages as an offering to the divinity that bears your name. O most beneficent and inseparable companion of true virtue and greatness, if your modesty derives greater pleasure from meriting than from receiving the sacrificial offerings of others, accept and be served at least by my appearance before you. In the name of all those of our sex I offer the present defense of women's worth to you, a princess of such vast power and dominion that you alone could defend the justice of this cause, not only against Signor Buoninsegni but even against the entire world. And, because I am aware of the rancor that many men direct toward women, which is known to me clearly through their writings, I wondered if I should place this offspring of my feeble mind under the protection of any one of them. Then suddenly Fame came with resounding voice, exclaiming the praises of your almost divine qualities, and immediately sent me running to place with great reverence these most imperfect strokes of my pen in the protective shade of your most famous golden oak tree.[3] I well know I am being rash, for which I beg that your regal kindness, which all acclaim to be incomparable, since you are a new Esther (not inferior to her in beauty, greatness or goodness), by means of the power you hold, will intervene and save your entire sex from unmerited prejudice, as she interceded to save all her people.[4] This has been the Daedalus that has given flight to the Icarus wings of my great desire, and so I do not fear a precipitous fall but hope for glory.

To you, therefore I turn, demigoddess of Tuscany, indeed of the entire universe, asking you to be my shield and protect me from the malevolent bite of the snarling critics who attack and wish to wound me. And who is it who would have the temerity to strike out at me when he sees himself confronted with so great

3. A reference to the Grand Duchess's family name Della Rovere, meaning "of the oak tree."

4. Esther, the biblical heroine of the Book of Esther, the beautiful Jewess married to King Ahasuerus, who saved her people who had been betrayed by Haman. Her story and those of other biblical heroines like Judith and Jael were popular subjects of painting and theater in the late sixteenth and early seventeenth century, as in, for example, the paintings of biblical heroines by Artemisia Gentileschi (1593–1652), and the plays of Federico Della Valle (c. 1560–1628) and Jean Racine (1639–1699).

a defense? The Aristarchuses[5] will be mute, the ignorant will be silent; the wise will understand, and Signor Buoninsegni himself will have the glorious fortune of being opposed by one who was not so imprudent to appear in battle without the patronage of that grand lady, to whom it was his happy lot to be born subject and servant. For now, if you will look upon and receive my homage favorably, I will proudly proclaim that in this fight I have won for myself a most glorious VITTORIA [victory]. Do not disdain, then, O most generous lady, to share the favor of your protection and defend the universal cause of all worthy women, and, as for me in particular, I most humbly beg you to pardon my excessive presumption. But perhaps I offend you when I underestimate your extraordinary kindness and grace, since you are the sum of all graces, or rather, to put it better, you are an immense ocean of every grace. Omnipotent God has given you a marvelous endowment, having made you the embodiment of all perfections and enriched you with all the things of greatest value that were created by his divine hand. Besides belonging to the sex that is dearest to Heaven, you are born of the most glorious lineage that has ever brightened the world, and you have joined in matrimonial bond with the most worthy ruler who wields the scepter of state.[6]

But these are only the smallest droplets of the vast sea of your merit and of your greatness, and so, fearful that the frail bark of my unpolished discourse will be engulfed in such a profound sea, I will leave it to the voices of all to proclaim your fame eternally. And what would the unlettered pen of one whose mind is dumbfounded by such wonders know to say about your countless superhuman qualities? Certainly nothing, since this would be material to tire the tongue and arms of the most famous orators and the celebrated historians of Greek and Roman eloquence. I will say then only that you are a wife worthy of that most serene ruler, the least attribute of whose worth is expressed in the title of grand, and, here, begging you for just a small share of your protective shade, I offer to pray God always for you, ceaselessly, however unworthily, that He grant you all the prosperity and greatness one can enjoy down here on this lowly earth, on which, I bow and humbly kiss Your Serene Highness' garments.

Venice, June 30, 1644

from the humble and most devoted servant
of Your Most Serene Highness,
A. T.

5. Aristarchus of Samothrace (c. 217–145 BCE), member of the school of Alexandria, Greek critic and grammarian, whose extensive work editing the Homeric poems made his name synonymous with that of critic.

6. Ferdinando II de' Medici (1610–1670), Grand Duke of Tuscany (1639–1670), married to Vittoria della Rovere in 1621.

Figure 4. Double portrait of Vittoria della Rovere and Grand Duke Ferdinando II de' Medici, by Justus Sustermans (1597–1681). © National Gallery, London / Art Resource, NY.

For Her Most Serene Highness
VITTORIA
Medici della Rovere
Grand Duchess of Tuscany
DEDICATION[7]

Queen of the Arno, whose exalted position
Brings another world under Tuscany's flag,
And so, with marvels flowing from your breast,
Among women of high rank you enjoy first place.
From the merciless empire's two tyrants,
Destructive time and profound oblivion,
I hide in the shade of your oak tree,
Where I hope to save this offspring of mine.
If in time a common oak can hold its own against
Sacred Jove, how much value must that oak
have that extends its branches in seven worlds?[8]
Ah, because your great name, already a winner,
Sounds a VITTORIA [victory] and it defends mine,
Your regal foilage brings with it civic honor.[9]

Regina d'Arno, il cui bel pregio altero
Cresce a la Tosca insegna un altro mondo,
Poiché, di meraviglie il sen fecondo,
Hai fra donne regal l'onor primiero.
Dei duo tiranni a lo spietato impero,
Tempo distruggitor e oblio profondo,
Mentre fra l'ombre di tua quercia ascondo,
Questo mio parto di sottrar io spero.
Se a Giove sacra con l'età contende
Quercia volgar, quanto aver die valore:
Quella che in sette mondi i rami stende?
Ah, che 'l bel nome tuo già vincitore
Suona VITTORIA e perché 'l mio diffende,
Torna il crine regal civico onore.

TO THE AUTHOR

O consort and handmaid of Celestial Love,
Since A[rcangela] is your name and you
Resemble the eternal gods,
You have certainly come down to us
From the precincts of the blessed.
But, if your every word seems like a star,
So too the paper where your words gather
Resembles not pages but the heavens above.

Scesa quaggiú ben sei,
O del celeste Amor sposa ed ancella,
Poiché nome hai d'A[rcangela] e sembiante
De' sempiterni Dei
Da le contrade sante.
Ma s'ogni detto tuo sembra una stella,
Cosí le carte, ove i tuoi detti accogli,
Sembran cieli e non fogli.

D[on] G[iovanni] B[attista] [di] S[ettimo][10]

7. The author of this dedicatory poem, *Regina d'Arno, il cui bel pregio altero* (published in Buoninsegni and Tarabotti, *Satira e Antisatira*, 34) is Andrea Valier (1615–1691), Venetian senator, general, historian and poet, a member of an illustrious Venetian family and correspondent of Tarabotti's. See Tarabotti, *Letters*, 125–26 (letter 72).

8. Meaning that the fame of the Rovere family extended through the entire universe, thought then to be consitituted by seven planets: Mercury, Venus, Mars, Jupiter, Saturn, the sun and the moon.

9. "il crin regal," which I have translated "regal foliage," is a reference to the oak leaves on the Della Rovere coat of arms.

10. Don Giovanni Battista di Settimo, the author of this madrigal, born in Palermo, was active in Venice, Padua, and Modena in the mid-seventeenth century. He belonged to the Venetian Academy

THE PRINTER TO THE READERS

If among the Spartans those were praised who hid their thefts, I should deserve great blame, for, instead of hiding this little work which I have stolen, I bring it to light in the world. The author who wrote it is lady A[rcangela] T[arabotti]. I refer to that A[rcangela] who only knew how to create paradises.[11] She wrote this *Antisatire* to please certain ladies, who knew they could to great advantage respond to the *Satire* of Buoninsegni and win in this contest with men if they could enlist the great talent of this one woman. Yet she disparages this work of hers, because, having a divine intellect, she cannot but abhor all things that are done out of necessity. I tried to persuade her to allow me to publish it, but she always refused, acting contrary to other women, who, in order to gain affection for their offspring, make nature appear more beautiful through art; this woman, because of her natural modesty, through artifice misrepresents her offspring to keep me from feeling affection for it. Finally, unable to obtain it through persuasion, I managed to steal it from one who had the good fortune to see it in manuscript.[12] Do not condemn me, my reader, because I am of the opinion that the ancients named Mercury the god of both rhetoric and theft to show that these activities must work together for their mutual benefit when necessary. I know that when this work appears she will be greatly offended, but I hope you will defend me, since the reason for this theft is equally the desire to do honor to my publications and my ardent wish to be of benefit to you. If you hear that she turns against me, declare yourselves in my favor, because in the end the world has a greater obligation to one who reveals treasures than to one who hides them. I have resolved on this occasion to reprint the *Satire*, because one cannot be a good judge of a dispute in which the vanities of women are condemned without seeing both the prosecution and the defense. Kindly accept, then, my offer of this little work and enjoy it until her other compositions appear in print; but, believe me, the only difference between this one and the others is that this is a small miracle and those will be great marvels. Be well.

---

of the Incogniti and corresponded with Giovan Francesco Loredan. The identification of the author was made by Apostolo Zeno on his copy of this work, held today at the Marciana Library in Venice.

11. A reference to *Convent Paradise,* a long treatise written by Tarabotti and published shortly before this work in Venice in 1643. See Introduction, 9, 10, and note 26.

12. According to Angelico Aprosio both he and Giacomo Pighetti, Tarabotti's brother-in-law, had seen the manuscript of the *Antisatire* (Aprosio, *La Biblioteca aprosiana*, 168, and Tarabotti, *Letters*, 172–175 (letter 122), and it is likely that other members of the Academy of the Incogniti, especially Giovanni Francesco Loredan, had seen it as well.

Against the Vanities of Women, a Menippean Satire
by Francesco Buoninsegni

Ladies, and all who the fair sex esteem,	*Donne, e voi che le donne avete in pregio,*
For God's sake do not listen to this tale	*Per Dio non date a quest'istoria orecchia*[1]

said the Ferrarese poet, as an excuse for his slander and to avoid incurring the hatred of women whom he provoked with the story that you know. Since I have been assigned the punishment of having to reproach women for their superfluous attention to adornment, to save myself from being the target of the hate in their hearts and the sharp arrows of their tongues, I will excuse myself with those same lines,

Ladies, and all who the fair sex esteem,	*Donne, e voi che le donne avete in pregio,*
For God's sake do not listen to this tale.	*Per Dio non date a quest'istoria orecchia.*

Take this discourse to be a sick man's dream,[2] the delirium of an academician, the lamentation of married men, conceived and born in a wine-induced ebullience; at its delivery the midwife was not Lucina,[3] who helps women give birth, but Bacchus, who helps intellectuals miscarry.

I have assumed the burden of this censure, though I did not choose it; everyone else turned it down. It is only by acting alone that one can speak out against women and incur little harm and very slight danger: it matters little if a useless wit exposes himself to the ire of women. Today I am to be the victim sacrificed to the scorn of these ladies. And yet (well you know it) there is no scorn to match the scorn of women.[4] That was said by the great sage, who was driven mad by love

1. Ludovico Ariosto, *Orlando furioso* 28.3.1–2. Translations are from Ariosto, *Orlando furioso (The Frenzy of Orlando): A Romantic Epic*, trans. Barbara Reynolds, 2 vols. (London: Penguin, 1975, 1977). With this warning the narrator seeks to allay the objections of women to the misogynist novella narrated in canto 28, which demonstrates that it is impossible to find a faithful women.

2. *Aegri somnia*, a literary commonplace. See Petrarca, *The Triumph of Love: Chastitie: Death*, trans. Anna Hume (Edinburgh: Evan Tyler, 1644) 4.65–66: "What is our life if ought it bring of ease / a sick man's dreame, a fable told to please." (Ben è 'l viver mortal, che sì n'agrada, / sogno d'infermi e fola di romanzi!) Petrarca, *Triumphus cupidinis*, ed. Vinicio Pacca (Milan: Mondadori, 1996). See also Horace, *Ars poetica* 7.

3. Lucina was the goddess of childbirth in ancient Rome.

4. Ecclesiasticus 25:23: Et non est ira super iram mulieris (And there is no anger above the anger of a woman; Sirach 25:23). For biblical texts unless otherwise indicated I cite the Latin text of the Vulgate and the English Douay-Rheims translation.

and, because of women, turned to worshipping idols.[5] Yet it is to serve women that I have willingly accepted this task. Anyone else of greater intelligence than I, who might have been chosen for it, would have said and done worse to them. I, who have lesser wit, will not do much harm and, even if I wound them, I want them to know that my weapons are innocent—they are like Achilles's spear, they wound and heal at the same time.[6] It is because the weapons of academicians, since they make the names of others eternal in their writing, do them good by reproaching them, and in the very act itself of wounding them they provide the egg white with which to stanch the bleeding of the wounds they make.[7]

Those women who serve as honored emissaries of love because they have had bad experiences themselves and so feel compassion for others, have no limb stronger nor contrivance mightier with which to bend the hearts of young women than gems, gold, and garments. Ovid's story of Cephalus and Procris, Ariosto's novella of the cup, and, lastly, our Rafaella do not allow me to lie.[8] The latter, the Sibyl of lovers, whose oracles, like those of the goddess Themis,[9] are revered by women, one day, as she was teaching her Margherita about the pleasures of love, knew no argument more efficacious with which to arouse love in the heart of that girl than to persuade her to wear luxurious clothes. This was the first lesson with which that wise teacher indoctrinated the ingenuous mind of that lady. Beneath her beautiful clothes she placed the arrow of Love and she gave her to drink the first drops of her poison from this golden cup.

I am not saying that *lusso* (luxury) is *lussuria* (lust); a subtle grammarian, showing off his Latin skills, has justly observed that the word *lusso* is half of the word *lussuria*. Yet if *lusso* is not *rio* (evil), it is not *lussuria*.[10] Let Rafaella hold her tongue. Let the grammarian hold his tongue. The latter, a silly pedant of Minerva,

5. The great sage is Solomon. See 3 Regnum 11:3–8 (1 Kings 11:3–8), where the story of Solomon's wives, concubines, and his idolatry is told.

6. Achilles's sword (the sword of his father Peleus) that wounds and heals is mentioned in Ovid's *Remedia amoris* 47–48 and *Tristia* 5.15–6; see also Dante, *Inferno* 30.4–6.

7. Albumin was an ancient remedy used to treat wounds; it stopped the bleeding.

8. These examples would seem to prove the efficacy of the offer of precious gifts and money to seduce women. In the first part of the story of Cephalus and Procris (Ovid, *Metamorphoses* 7.661–865) the jealous Cephalus disguises himself and offers his unsuspecting wife a large amount of money and many gifts if she will betray her husband with him; when it seems she will accept, Cephalus reveals his identity. The story of the cup in the *Orlando furioso* (42.102–104; 43.9–46), like that of Cephalus, tells of a man who appeared to his wife disguised as another and tempted her successfully with an offer of precious gems. In Alessandro Piccolomini's dialogue *La Raffaella* (1539), the protagonist teaches a young girl to attract a lover by adorning herself with beautiful clothes, jewelry, and cosmetics.

9. In Aeschylus (*Eumenides* 2) the goddess who spoke through the Oracle of Delphi. See also Ovid, *Metamorphoses* 1.321.

10. Since this play on words is impossible to reproduce in English, I have left it in Italian and provide an English translation of the terms in parentheses.

and the former, a foolish pedant of Venus, do not understand. Love requires stability; vanity is its mortal enemy. Idleness is the father of Love, as the poet has told us:

Idleness gave him birth, and wantonness.	*Ei nacque d'ozio, e di lascivia umana.*[11]

And did the teacher of loves not also say

If you take away idleness, Cupid's bow is unstrung?	*Se togli l'ozio è senza strale Amore?*[12]

Bad news for lovers! Ladies occupied for an entire year in arranging an elaborate hair style have no leisure time to make love.

But it is futile to think we can convince women not to let their vanity govern how they dress, if we first fail to disrobe them of ignorance. They adorn their bodies with pompous regal robes, as though they are so many suns at the Gate of the East

Adorned in celestial	*Per accrescer adorne*
Splendors to add	*Di celesti splendori*
Luster to the Sun, joy to the world, and fire to hearts.	*Lume al sol, gioia al mondo, e fiamme a' cori.*[13]

And they are unaware that such a dark cloud of ignorance obscures their minds.

Loveliest ladies, what do you think these pompous garments are that you find so fascinating, so delightful to your eyes? They are nothing more than the most obvious testimony to your enslavement and the punishment you deserve for your Edenic sin. The guilt that deprived our first parents of the clothing of innocence also opened their eyes to their nakedness. The air poisoned by the breath of the infernal snake turned harshly against those who disobeyed the divine commandment. The shame of their nakedness and the ire of Heaven made it necessary for them to wear clothes. Today feminine vainglory has turned necessity into arrogance and woman, taking great pride in the sign of her servitude, now doubly guilty, has turned the punishment of her sin into a triumph of luxury.

11. Petrarch, the poet *par excellence*, *Trionfo d'amore* 1.82. *The Triumphs of Petrarch*, trans. Ernest Hatch Wilkins (Chicago: University of Chicago Press, 1962).

12. Ovid, *Remedia amoris* 139: Otia si tollas, periere Cupidinis arcus. See the bilingual edition Ovid, *The Art of Love and Other Poems*, trans. J. H. Mozley, 2nd ed., revised by G. P. Goold (Cambridge, MA: Harvard University Press; London: William Heinemann, 1979), 186.

13. Buoninsegni is probably the author of these unattributed lines.

These garments are spun of silk, which in the end is nothing more that the vomit and sepulcher of a worm. Our poet says this in a sonnet on the silkworm:[14]

This fertile seed of another's pomp,	*Questo del fasto altrui gravido seme,*
Animate treasure, living atom,	*Animato tesoro, atomo vivo,*
Fears not to be born in a lady's lascivious breast	*Di donzella gentil nel sen lascivo,*
Where others go mad and die.	*Dove folle altrui muor, nascer non teme.*
It feeds itself on leaves and men on hope,	*Pasce al par sé di foglie e l'uom di speme,*
It sleeps and sometimes wakes but cannot see,	*Dorme e veglia talor de gli occhi privo,*
It builds its tomb and half alive still	*Fabbrica la sua tomba e semivivo*
In its last hours brings riches to its burial.	*Arricchisce l'essequie a l'ore estreme.*
A tiny phoenix at whose death is reborn;	*Pargoletta fenice al fin rinasce;*
For then of its remains an industrious hand	*Quindi de le sue spoglie industre mano*
Weaves silken cloaks and regal wraps.	*Tesse serici ammanti e regie fasce.*
Now why does the ambitious heart in vain	*Or perché tanto insuperbisce in vano*
Swell up with pride if human pomp is born	*Ambizioso il cor, se solo nasce*
From nothing more than the tomb of a worm?	*Dal sepolcro d'un verme il fasto umano!*

So woman is nothing more than a worm that devours the heart of lovers, a delicate vomit of nature, and a gilded tomb of human hearts.

These silks dyed with the innocent blood of animals are all poisoned.[15] They are Deianira's woven garment, poisoned by the centaur's blood.[16] There is only one

14. When he writes "our poet" (il nostro poeta) Buoninsegni is referring to himself. This sonnet is included among his works in two manuscripts at the National Library in Florence (BNCF, Palatino 263, fols. 76v–77r, and Magliabechi VII 456, fol. 26r. See Introduction, 15). It is published in Melchor i Fenollosa, "Sonets esparsos," 80. The poem was erroneously attributed instead to Ciro di Pers in the 1672 edition of his poetry; however, the editor of that collection included a note to the reader in which he acknowledged the error. This error has been repeated in the modern edition Ciro di Pers, *Poesie*, ed. Michele Rak (Turin: Einaudi, 1978).

15. The "sangue innocente degli animali" (innocent blood of animals) is a case of hypallage or transferred epithet, meaning the blood of innocent animals.

16. Buoninsegni refers to the story of the tunic, dyed with the poisonous blood of the centaur Nessus, that Deianira made and gave to Hercules, thinking it would make him faithful to her, as Nessus promised. Instead it clung to Hercules, made him suffer terribly, and eventually killed him. Buoninsegni seems to know the version of the story recounted by Sophocles in *The Women of Trachis*, where the tunic is said to have been woven by Deianira, and he undoubtedly also knew the versions in Ovid's *Heroides* and *Metamorphoses* 9.98ff.

difference between these silks and that garment, and it is that the latter poisoned only the one who put it on, and the former do not kill the women who wear them (too bad) but their husbands who buy them and the lovers who admire them. How many there are who, struck more by the splendor of the clothes their ladies wear than by the light of their eyes, fall more for their dresses than for their ladies' faces. They adore them in the churches, they follow them in the streets, they court them in the public squares, and they serve them at parties; they act as their footmen all day leading and following their carriages, and then, when the ladies return home to take off their dresses (and it would then complete their service to accompany them to their rooms), they abandon them discourteously at the doorstep. This complaint is expounded heroically by an offended lady poet in a long and lovely madrigal that goes

Let's each take up the arms of scorn for men	*Contro gli uomini ognuna armi lo sdegno,*
Since they want nothing more than	*Che loro solo bramano*
To see our beautiful clothes; they don't love us:	*Veder le belle vesti e noi non amano:*
When we take off our covering	*Ad ispogliarne il guscio*
Of these beautiful clothes,	*Di queste belle vesti,*
When we enter the house,	*A la soglia de l'uscio*
They stop and stand apart outside,	*Fermati in un cantone,*
Like a guard at the door.	*Ci fanno un bel piantone.*
This is a clear sign indeed	*Quest'è pur chiaro segno*
That, if they are so quick to leave us,	*Che, se sono cosí pronti a lasciarne,*
They love not our bodies but our clothes	*Amano in noi le vesti e non la carne.*[17]

Now what shall we say about the great a variety of colors that they wear? Truly in this women betray themselves and their beauty. As the proverb says:

The color black is makeup for a lady's face.	*Il liscio de le donne è il color nero.*[18]

How is that? Can the symbol of death give life to beauty? Yes, sir, it is because black attracts one's sight, and the eye, abhorring to look at something so depressing, turns its gaze entirely on the face; whereas, if one's sight is distracted by the variety of the other colors, the face loses out, since it does not get all of the attention of the

17. Tarabotti in her response to this satire denies that a woman could have written these lines. I have not found a source for them and believe they were probably written by Buoninsegni himself, since they correspond exactly to what he has said in the prose passage that precedes them.

18. On this passage and proverb, see Massimo Baldini, Marica Spalletti, and Maria Vittoria Adelman, eds., *La moda capelli: La storia, le teorie e i dati di tipo visuale* (Rome: Armando, 2006), 28.

gaze of others. If, therefore, a woman is more beautiful in clothes that are dark and not in colors, her beauty gains from another's loss of life.[19]

But let us allow woman alone to adorn herself from head to foot, since she was created to provide respite to man after his travails. Why though should a woman made of flesh be half clothed as a woman of wood (fig. 5)? I do not complain about the height of her wooden shoes. It is not my charge. Let them have shoes so high that women look like princesses and deserve to be called Your Highness. It matters little. But it is not good to spend so much money to dress inanimate wood.[20] A dressmaker would need only half as much brocade to cover just the part that is flesh. Go ahead, let the hem of the garment reach but not go further than the top of the shoes, and then make them as high as a pike (figs. 6 and 7).[21]

It will make quite a holy spectacle one day	*Sarà pure un spettacolo divino*
To see you, your clothes hiked up half way,	*Vedervi alzate a mezza gamba un giorno,*
With two wooden legs and brocade drapery	*Far, con le vesti di broccato intorno,*
Looking like a religious ceremonial canopy.	*A due gambe di legno il baldachino.*[22]

Now it is, yes, gentlemen, that I fear the vessel of my wits is about to break apart and sink, not in the Strait of Messina between Scylla and Charybdis,

But between two cliffs of wood	*Ma nel mar de lo sdegno*
In this scorn-filled sea.	*Fra due scogli di legno.*

Well, since ladies are amiable there is no danger that I will be destroyed. And then mine is the ship of Ulysses; it will sail by safely through the strait dominated by this lighthouse tower.[23] I fear, however, that if I sail in my ship, these ladies will

19. This bizarre pseudoscientific argument means that a lady dressed in black attracts attention to her face, since the eye prefers not to look at black, which is too depressing, and that the many colors of clothes, pleasing to look at, would instead distract the gaze from the woman's face. This is a gain for the lady, who feels more beautiful since her face is admired, and what her beauty gains is at the expense of other life—that is, the death mourned by dressing in black.

20. Buoninsegni here objects that a woman's clothing covers not only her body, but also must cover the tall shoes she wears—the *pianelle*, the very tall wooden platform shoes also known as *zoccoli*, *calcagnini*, or *calcagnetti*.

21. *Una picca*, an infantry weapon consisting of a metal spearhead on a long wooden shaft.

22. These lines are by Buoninsegni. He refers to them in another satire he wrote later on the foolishness of men, the *Delle sciocchezze degli huomini*: "E dissi O che spettacolo divino / Saria vederle inalborate un giorno / Far con la veste di broccato intorno / A due gambe di legno il baldacchino." BNCF, Magl. VII 456, fol. 55r, lines 5–8 in a fair copy; fol. 100r, lines 5–8 in an autograph manuscript. See Introduction, 24, and note 71.

23. Buoninsegni's reference to the lighthouse continues the metaphor with which he describes passing through the wooden legs of a lady wearing high wooden shoes as though through a passage of water like the Strait of Messina where a lighthouse tower stands.

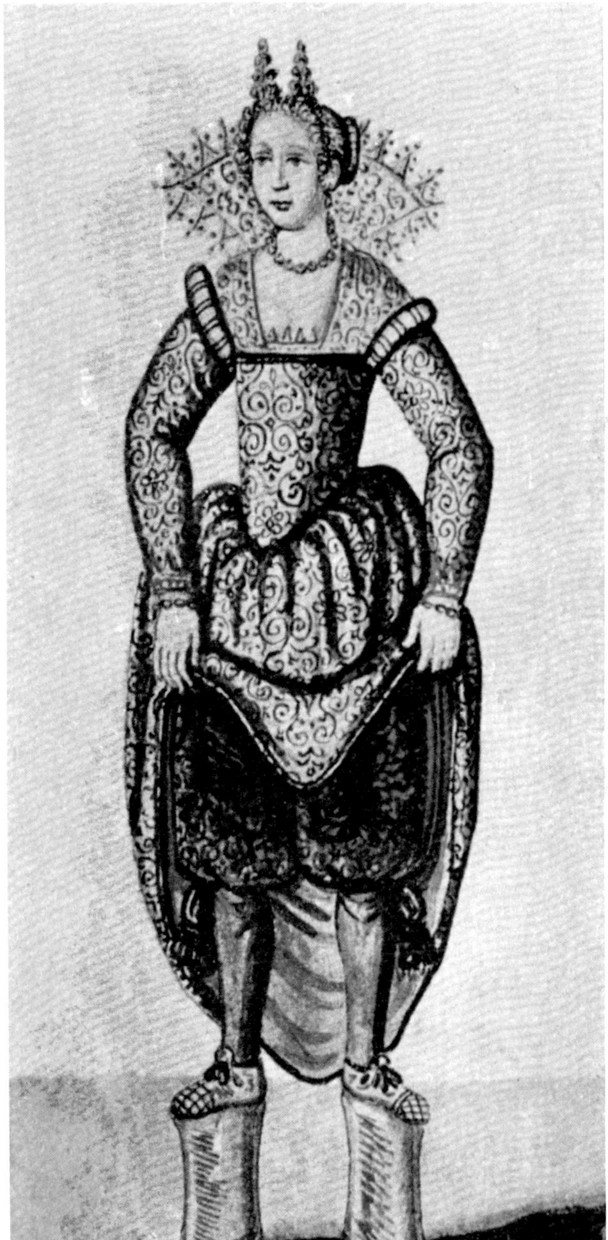

Figure 5. Lady "baldachin," from E. Rodocanachi, *La femme italienne à l'époque de la Renaissance* (Paris: Hachette, 1907). Courtesy of the University of Chicago Library.

Figure 6. *Pianelle*, Venetian platform shoes, seventeenth century. Museum of Fine Arts, Boston.

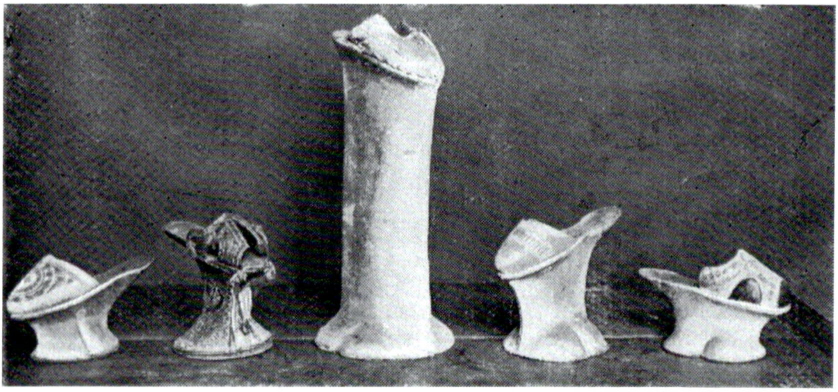

Figure 7. *Pianelle*, Venetian platform shoes, sixteenth and seventeenth century. Musée de Cluny, Paris.

not have Ulysses's wax in their ears. They have merchants' ears.[24] Let's open them better, since the weight of the heavy earrings they wear pull down on them but do not do their job of keeping them open very well. I am certain to be hit with their wooden shoes, but I do not fear finding out how hard they are, even knowing how big they are. Because the shoes are so heavy, ladies have more strength in their legs to drag along in them than they have in their arms to hurl them.

Without a doubt women will eventually all be transformed into trees and we will need a new Ovid to take care of them in an addition to his *Metamorphoses*. A third of their body is already wooden. The metamorphoses of all those who have been turned into trees began from their feet and not their head. Listen to the transformation of Dryope[25] who was one of them:

And as she turns her body[26] and her head	*E nel girar del corpo e de la testa*
She feels a root holding her foot down.	*Sente che una radice il piè gli arresta.*
She tries, she struggles to lift her foot	*D'alzar pur ella il piè si prova e sforza,*
But the greedy earth will not allow it;	*Ma comportar nol vuol l'avida terra;*
Already new wood and unwanted bark	*Già il nuovo legno e l'importuna scorza*
Hide and seal her legs within a trunk.	*Le gambe in un troncon nasconde e serra.*

Her wooden nature having grown little by little, when it reaches her mouth, she says:

Dear husband of mine, mother,[27] sister too,	*Dolce consorte mio, madre, e sorella,*
Receive from me my last goodbye,	*Da me prendete l'ultimo saluto,*
For already I feel my speech held back	*Che già mancar mi sento la favella*
By the tree that has grown too far in me.	*Per l'arbore che troppo è in me cresciuto.*

If now you see before your eyes one of these ladies with so many beautiful dresses, so many necklaces, being transformed into a tree, will she not seem to be precisely

24. They won't miss anything. Their ears will be open.

25. Ovid, *Metamorphoses* 9.324–93, the story of Dryope, turned into a tree for having picked flowers of the water lotus, the metamorphosed form of the naiad Lotis. Buoninsegni cites from Ovid using the Italian translation in narrative octaves by Giovanni Andrea dell'Anguillara (1517–1565), but he makes a few linguistic changes. Moreover, the lines he takes from dell'Anguillara are not consecutive, as the quoted passage would make it seem. They are precisely 9.138.7–8 and 139.1–2, 5–6, corresponding to *Metamorphoses* 9.139–53. See *Le metamorfosi d'Ovidio, ridatte da Giovanni Andrea dell'Anguillara in ottava rima* (Milan: Dalla Società tipografica de' classici italiani, 1805).

26. All of the published editions of Buoninsegni's satire (including this one, published together with Tarabotti's response) have the word *capo* (head) here, an obvious error for *corpo* (body), the reading in the dell'Anguillara translation; *Le metamorfosi d'Ovidio*, 9.138.7. I have made the correction.

27. In both Ovid and in dell'Anguillara's translation, Dryope calls out to her father, not her mother, as she does here. See Ovid, *Metamorphoses* 9.382, 388–89; *Le metamorfosi d'Ovidio*, 148.1–4.

the plane tree of Lydia, with its regal mantle that Xerxes in a moment of madness crowned with a golden diadem?[28] If now we actually saw one of these metamorphoses, could we believe that all the hair on their heads would be changed into leaves? I do not think so. How many are the wigs they wear that have nothing in them that belongs to the *anima vegetativa*![29] Enter stage the Satyr of the *Faithful Shepherd* with hairpiece in hand—not Corisca's, but that of a cadaver, despoiled in the tomb;[30] and if you find this hard to believe, just take my word for it!

But my discourse, like a bird, has lithely hopped from foot to head, from pillar to post, on the top of the trees, and, without realizing it, I have left the ladies with their shoes uncovered. Let them cover up as they will, surround their wooden fortress with a bulwark of silk and gold, and, as they walk down the streets where ball games are being played, let us hope the tragic fate of the Colossus of Nebuchadnezzar, King of Babylon, not befall them.[31] However, their shoes being made of gold and silver, one could say these ladies were that statue upside down, with golden feet and a wooden head.[32] But how can we say a wooden head? That chin of ivory, shaped in the workshop of Minerva?[33] That mouth, where laughter reigns, whose smile[34] reveals the harmony of Paradise? That nose, a tower, not David's but of Babel, where the most esteemed orators contend raising their voices in praise? Those rosy cheeks colored rather by the blood of a thousand hearts, not by that from Venus's foot?[35] Those ears, two labyrinths of Love, where the prayers

28. Herodotus, *Histories* 7.31.

29. For Aristotle, in *On the Soul*, the part of the soul that is the *anima vegetativa* is its nutritive power which belongs to both animals and plants. Buoninsegni here means to say that there is nothing natural about women's hair. It is not their living hair: they are wearing wigs.

30. The reference is to Battista Guarini's pastoral drama the *Pastor fido*, act 2, scene 6, in which the Satyr tries to capture the nymph Corisca grabbing her by the hair, but the nymph, who was wearing a wig, escapes, leaving the Satyr with the wig in his hand. The theme of Guarini's scene and Buoninsegni's passage is the vanity and falsity of women. Buoninsegni's reference to wigs made from the hair of the dead picks up on the words of Guarini's Satyr: "[malvagia incantatrice…] i sepolcri spoglia / e, dai fracidi teschi il crin furando" ([a wicked enchantress…] empties the tombs / and steals hair from the rotting heads). Battista Guarini, *Il pastor fido*, ed. Elisabetta Selmi (Venice: Marsilio, 1999), lines 990–91.

31. Daniel 2:31–35. The colossus that came to Nebuchadnezzar in a dream was hit by a stone, fell, and was completely destroyed. This colossal statue had a head of gold, silver trunk and arms, bronze belly and thighs, iron legs, and feet part iron part clay.

32. No part of the biblical colossus was made of wood.

33. Minerva, Roman goddess of the arts, including science, and handicrafts, and later of war.

34. I accept the reading "denti" (teeth) found in the editions of 1638 and 1644 V1; however, the edition of 1644 V2 introduces a variant reading "detti" (speech or words) which is also repeated in the edition of 1656. Since the description is otherwise a list of specific body parts, I believe the reference to the lady's teeth more likely. I have translated the expression, however, with a synecdoche: smile.

35. Venus's foot was pricked by a rose's thorn. This is perhaps a reference to the scene in Giambattista Marino's *L'Adone*, canto 3, octave 118.

of lovers are lost? Those eyes, a summation, a quintessence of the stars distilled by Aesculapius?[36] Those eyebrows, two rainbows dressed darkly to mourn the death of their marvelous mother?[37] That hair, sphere of the Sun, spun by the hands of the Graces? And, lastly, that entire face, a drawing and a stroke of the Divine brush? These things made of wood?

All these things made of wood? Gentlemen, no. A woman's head, gentlemen, yes. The head of a woman is not what we see on her neck. The head of a woman is a man, a head truly wooden to allow the gold and silver—mined by human greed in the bowels of hell at the expense of so many lives—to be condemned to lie beneath the feet of a woman. This would be to subject them to the miserable fate of the golden basins belonging to that Roman lady, about whom, if you are curious enough to want to know of such a misfortune, you should ask Martial, who will tell you in that very amusing couplet that goes

You empty your stomach shamelessly into a golden pot,	*Ventris onus misero (nec te pudet) excipis auro*
Bassa, ...	*Bassa*. . . . . [38]

I forgot the rest. If any one of these gentlemen who are listening to me knows it, let him kindly tell us. He will acquire for life the honor of being remembered by me; and let him recite the missing pentameter line of that most beautiful couplet to these gentle ladies, who will be happy to hear it.

Let us now move on from these statues with feet of gold, so that if they fall they will not land on top of us, and let us return to rest beneath our trees, even though they will not give us much shade since they do not have a lot of leaves. As I said, not all the hair will have been transformed into leaves. Yesterday morning a gentleman and friend of mine was calling for the housemaid when his wife said: "Leave her be. She is in my bedroom arranging my hair. I am invited to the Academy on Sunday, and I want to go with a new and unusual hair style." "Go ahead," said her husband, "I hope those academicians will give it a good dressing

36. Aesculapius was the god of medicine for the Greeks and then for the Romans. Ancient science considered the earth, water, air, and fire the four elements of which the world was made. According to Aristotle and the Pythagoreans, the fifth element, or quintessence, was ether, of which the celestial bodies were formed. Buoninsegni uses the term in its alchemical meaning of the purest part.

37. The goddess of the rainbow is Iris, daughter of the cloud nymph Electra and Thaumas, a marine god.

38. Buoninsegni cites the Latin passage but leaves the more vulgar part of the second line incomplete. The couplet is by the first-century CE Roman poet Martial, *Epigrammaton* 1.37: Ventris onus misero, nec te pudet, excipis auro, / Bassa, bibis vitro. Carius ergo cacas. *M. Valerii Martialis Epigrammaton libri*, ed. Ludwig Friedlaender, 2 vols. (Leipzig: S. Hirzel, 1886). In my literal translation: You empty your stomach shamelessly into a golden pot, / Bassa, while you drink from a glass. You spend more to defecate.

down." "There is no danger of this," she replied, "because those academicians only know how to say kind things. They are unable to produce bad comments of this sort;[39] they leave them to courtiers for whom speaking ill of others is a special talent." "That is true," her husband replied, "but you, dear wife, tell me, as you live and breathe, how many heads do you have? Either you are the hydra of Hercules,[40] or, while you are here beside me, you have your head elsewhere." And, as he was saying this, he entered her room and found the maid wrapping a string of oriental pearls around some rags and a hemp cord (fig. 8).[41]

Astonished by what he saw, the husband, as though he had seen the head of Medusa, said "This is just what we needed! For the price of a hundred bushels of grain that I bought this year from Checchi and Marchi[42] to support your extravagances and then had to sell at two miserable *carlini*[43] a sack, given my need and the abundance of wheat in the glutted city market! And the price, I tell you, of all that grain was certainly ill spent to dress up four handlengths of rags!"[44]

Cato, that great Censor of Roman pomp, in his time thought that Rome was near its final ruin when he heard that the selling price of a fish was the same as that

39. Literally, their offspring (*parti*) of this sort of speech are miscarriages (*sconciature*); i.e., they are not carried through but are aborted. Birth metaphors for literary production, bad and good, are commonplace in this period. There are many examples in the works of Tarabotti, Aprosio, and Loredan, nor was the practice limited to members of that circle. See, for example, Torquato Accetto, *Della dissimulazione onesta* 15.1, and Traiano Boccalini, *Ragguagli di Parnaso* 31.3.

40. The Hydra of Lerna, killed by Hercules, had nine heads.

41. Women's hairstyles in the seventeenth century were large constructions adorned with ties, ribbons, and bows; the more expensive and ostentatious ones were also ornamented with pearls. On seventeenth-century hair styles see Levi-Pisetzky, "Il gusto barocco," 84–85, and Levi-Pisetzky, *Storia del costume*, 324–408. See also *Recueil général de coeffures de différents gouts, ou l'on voit la manière dont se coëffoient les femmes, sous différents règnes, à commencer en 1589 jusqu'en 1778* (Paris: Desnos, 1778).

42. Common names, used here generically to indicate buying from one or another of various merchants.

43. *Carlino*, a small silver coin used in everyday exchange, so named because it was initially minted in Naples by Charles I d'Anjou (Carlo d'Angiò) in the late thirteenth century. The term was later used throughout Italy for coins that were worth about half a *lira*, and there were 7 *lire* in a *scudo* or a ducat. According to Carlo Cipolla a *staio* (here translated as "sack") of wheat in seventeenth-century Italy cost about 1.08 *scudi*. Carlo M. Cipolla, *Fighting the Plague in Seventeenth-Century Italy* (Madison: University of Wisconsin Press, 1981), 68n36. Thus the husband got only "two miserable carlini" for each sack when he should have expected around 14 or 15.

44. I have translated the Italian measure *moggia* (plural of *moggio*) as bushels, though a *moggio* was somewhat larger than a bushel; and *staia* (plural of *staio*) as sacks, to indicate a smaller amount: 1 *moggio* was equal to 24 *staia* and there is another Italian measurement, *sacco* or *sacca*, slightly larger than a *staio* (1 *sacco* = 3 *staia*). I could find no exact equivalents for these terms in English and have chosen to suggest the proportion of one to the other. I thank Sharon Strocchia for her help with these measurements.

of an ox.[45] Oh poor Cato! And what would you say if you came back in these times and saw not a mullet, which at least one can eat, but an eel made of rags on the head of my wife that is worth the price of a hundred oxen? Truly this hemp cord would better fulfill the function nature gave it than the one you force on it through artifice, if it served not as an ornament but as a remedy for your feeble brain.[46]

Figure 8. Nicolas Arnoult, *Femme de qualité estant à sa toilette* (1688). Bibliothèque nationale de France (also see figs. 1 and 2).

45. Marcus Porcius Cato (234–149 BCE), Roman statesman, elected to the censorship in 184 BCE. For this anecdote see the life of Cato in Plutarch's *Parallel Lives*.

46. That is to say, it would better serve as a noose.

Pearls and salt are born of the same father: both are offspring of the sea. That is as it should be. One whose wits lack salt puts on pearls; and one who has nothing precious in his brain looks outside to remedy what inside is missing. Our poet[47] on this subject expressed it well:

The bodies of the ladies	*I corpi delle donne*
Who rush off to parties	*Che corrono alla festa*
In gowns so lavish,	*Con cosí riche gonne,*
And so many jewels in their hair,	*Con tante gioie in testa,*
Are like huts made of hay,	*Son cappanne di fieno,*
Covered (strange to behold!)	*Coperte con pazzissimo lavoro*
By roof tiles of pearls and gutters of gold.	*Da tegole di perle e docci d'oro.*

A woman's head with so many remarkable figures constructed on it looks to me like a deck of playing cards. A perfect comparison. Ask these gentlemen who play cards about it and they will say (especially when they lose) that the cards and (I add) women have rags for brains. And yours in particular would not be one of those figures that they call the World and the Triumphs but rather the one they call the Tarot card Fool.[48] Would you like to see the four suits in this deck of cards?[49] Coins (*denari*) are there but ill spent on so many jewels. Swords (*spade*) are not lacking; every woman so that she looks like Pallas, the armed goddess of wisdom, must have her little silver sword.[50] Clubs (*bastoni*) are worn hidden beneath the curls and, even though they are not visible to the eye, the proof that they are there is in the coffers which take a hit for the pomp they support.[51] Whence our good-natured poet said:[52]

A lady would die if she could not always wear	*La donna muor se non ha sempre tutto*
Her husband's net worth on her back,	*Del suo marito addosso il capitale,*
Whence both husband and fortune a sad end will share.	*Ond'è che questo e quello è mal condotto.*

That is to say, from the clubbing they get from the hard head of their wives. Nor do the ladies lack cups (*coppe*). All they do is attach suction cups to their husbands'

47. Buoninsegni, see notes 13, 14, 17, 22 above.

48. The World, the Triumphs (also called the Chariot), and the Fool belong to the tarot Major Arcana. The first two have positive connotations while the Fool, as the name implies, does not.

49. The four suits listed are *danari* (coins), *spade* (swords), *bastoni* (clubs), and *coppe* (cups).

50. A pin to hold the hair in place.

51. Presumably, supports for the large constructed hairdo.

52. See note 47 above.

purses to draw what little blood is left there. And for those who play with French cards, look at the head of these ladies and see how many flowers (*fiori*) there are that were touched by King Midas's hand.[53] Hearts (*cuori*) are imprisoned there by the dozens; with each hair a heart is hanged. There are pikes (*picche*), quite long ones. How many lovers are piqued and, because the pique is long, are never satisfied![54] Ladies don't lack bricks either; they use heavy ones to punish their husbands.[55]

Neither flies nor women attended the sacrifices in the temple of Hercules. Flies, out of their natural instinct; women, forbidden by divine decree. The reason for the flies does not pertain to our discussion, except that nature itself and Heaven tell us that there is little difference between flies and women and that the saying "to go about chasing flies," a futile exercise, applies rightly to women.[56] The reason for excluding women is this. The statue of Hercules, when it came within the sight of Chios, could not be pulled into port with all the ropes on the island. When the god was asked the cause of his resistance, he answered that he wanted to be pulled to shore with a rope woven of women's hair. The women of Chios were not used to wearing wigs and went around looking lovely with their hair loose, and they did not want to comply. So it was to preserve their beauty that they committed an act of impiety, considering one hair to be worth more than a god.[57] Nor was this unreasonable: a woman's most beautiful ornament is her hair. Nymphs and goddesses prided themselves on this above all.

Her beautiful golden hair was streaming in the wind	*Erano i bei crin d'oro a l'aura sparsi,*[58]

53. Gold flowers. The suit Buoninsegni calls *fiori* (flowers) corresponds to the French suit of *trèfles*, more commonly known as clovers or clubs. The other French suits are *coeurs* (hearts), *piques* (pikes), and *carreaux* (diamonds or tiles).

54. Buoninsegni plays on the word "picche" (pikes), the French tarot suit corresponding to the Italian "spade" (swords), and the meaning in this context of the verb *piccarsi*, to take offense, or pique. I have had to use two variants, pikes (*picche*) and pique to approximate his word play.

55. Buoninsegni's mention of bricks (*mattoni*) is suggested by the French suit of *carreaux*, since *carreaux* also has the meaning of bricks. He then uses the Italian word for bricks, *mattoni*, in the idiomatic expression *dare il mattone*, meaning to hurt. I have translated it here as to punish.

56. The Italian expression "pigliar le mosche per aria," which I have translated as "chasing flies," means chasing after vain ideas or futile things.

57. The anecdote comes from Pausanias and was recounted by Vincenzo Cartari in the sixteenth century in *Le immagini de i dei degli antichi* (1556), chapter 9. I thank Paolo Cherchi for this reference, for which see the modern Italian edition Vincenzo Cartari, *Le immagini de i dei degli antichi*, ed. Ginetta Auzzas, Federica Martignago, Manlio Pastore Stocchi, and Paola Rigo (Vincenza: Neri Pozza, 1996), 311–12.

58. Petrarch's famous line, but incorrectly remembered: "Erano i capei d'oro a l'aura sparsi," *Canzoniere (Rerum vulgarium fragmenta)* 90.1. Francesco Petrarca, *Canzoniere*, ed. Marco Santagata (Milan:

he said. Why adulterate such a precious thing with so many rags, so much idle rant?[59]

Charillus, a beautiful young Athenian boy, when asked why he grew his hair (listen and learn a manly response, vain yes, but a judicious vanity): "Because," he said, "this ornament belongs to me and it costs me nothing."[60] And you, gentle ladies, have your own ornaments that cost you nothing. Why do you spend money and ruin them?

Now, what shall we say of those ladies who, when they are old and have white hair, dye it? They do harm to their declining years when their hair color has finally become a symbol of innocence. And yet their white hair, like the rags in fig groves that scare away the birds, frightens off lovers.

And whom our furrows snow shall cover	*Ed a canuto e livido sembiante*
Love may return, but never lover.	*Può ben tornar amor, ma non amante.*[61]

The truth spoken by Corisca. On seeing his lady one morning, who in a hurry to leave the house had not tinted her hair as she normally did, our poet[62] did not leave her without saying to her:

Now upon the alpine heights of your white hair	*Già sovra l'alpi del tuo bianco crine*
The winter of your coldest years brings snow;	*De' piú fredd'anni incanutisce il verno;*
Now I see the springtime disappear	*Già sparir primavera e già discerno*
The roses fade and the thorns grow.	*Languir le rose e inrigidir le spine.*
The great theft of Time now takes your glory,	*Fa 'l tempo di tue glorie alte rapine,*
An eternal freeze shrouds my burning love;	*Copre il mio grave incendio un gelo eterno;*

Mondadori, 1996). The reference to Laura is alluded to in the expression "a l'aura," in the breeze.

59. With "so many rags" and "so much idle rant" I have attempted to render Buoninsegni's play on words "con tanti cenci, con tante ciance."

60. The account is taken from Lodovico Ricchieri (1450–1520), known as Celio Rhodigino, in his *Lectionum antiquarum libri XXX*, book 15, chapter 8. See Lodovico Ricchieri, *Charilaum interogatum cur coman nutriret, respondisse, Quoniam ex omni ornatu hic pulchrior foret, venustiorque, ac sumpus minimi* (Lyon: apud Sebastianum Honoratum, 1560), 315. I thank Paolo Cherchi for this reference.

61. Guarini, *Il pastor fido*, act 3, scene 5, lines 673–74. They are the words of the nymph Corisca. I have used the seventeenth-century English translation of this couplet by Sir Richard Fanshawe, *The Faithfull Shepherd* (1647), published in Guarini, *Il pastor fido*, ed. J. H. Whitfield (Austin: University of Texas Press, 1976), 211. Literally, the first line reads: to a [person] whitehaired and [of] pale appearance.

62. Buoninsegni. The sonnet is found in his verse collection, BNCF, Magl. VII 456, fol. 22r, and also in Magl. VII 369, fol. 244v. It is published in Melchor i Fenollosa, "Sonets esparsos," 82.

So for my comfort and your scorn	*Cosí per mio conforto e per tuo scherno*
My suffering and your splendor cease.	*Qui del mio strazio e del tuo fasto è 'l fine.*
Once it was (ah! to think of it yet	*Tempo già fu (ahi! che in pensarlo ancora*
makes my heart sigh) my mind worshipped	*Sospira il cor) che idolatrò mia mente*
your beauty at its borning dawn.	*Di tue bellezze alla nascente aurora.*
On the altar now my burning breast	*Or su l'altar di questo seno ardente*
will sacrifice no more, for it is no one	*Non piú vittime avrai che non adora,*
save a mad idolater adores the setting sun.	*Se non folle idolatra, il sol cadente.*

Women, who know they have this disadvantage in the eyes of men, to keep their lovers faithful dye their hair. And truly they outsmart the human condition (putting to shame the alchemists who blow on the fire all year to burn the wings of fleeting Mercury)[63] and with the most ingenious alchemy turn the quicksilver of white hair into streaming waves of gold.

The vanities of female ornamentation (like all the vanities in this world) are no more than shadows and their increase is a sign that the sun of your beauty, my gentle ladies, is setting among the dark shadows of your superfluous pomp.

The sun is without ornament,	*Senz' ornamento è 'l sole,*
The stars are simple forms:	*Son semplici le stelle:*
Your vanities, ladies, lessen your charms.	*Le vostre vanità vi fan men belle.*

And is it not true that fools think more of clothes than of the soul? The best dressed ladies are considered the most virtuous. It is a foolish thing to judge the value of a body by the length of the shadow it makes.

Gentlemen, I have finished my discourse without having even briefly considered the mirror and cosmetics, the principal instruments of feminine vanity. This is a clear sign that my discourse has not been painted and primped, nor has it mirrored itself in the mirror of eloquence, touched up with the cosmetics of artifice. It was appropriate that the discourse against the vanities appear without ornament.

Perhaps, therefore, I will not have been persuasive. This does not surprise me; my cause is hopeless. The belly has no ears, says an old adage that condemns gluttony.[64] Clothes have no ears: a new adage that denounces the vanities. I would need the voice of Orpheus to animate these senseless garments. I fear that the scorn

63. The alchemy of women who can transform their hair from silver to gold is better than that of Mercury. The reference is to mercury, or quicksilver, the prime matter that is "purified" in fire by alchemists in order to use it to transform base metals into gold. Mercury is said to be fleeting, a symbol of time and messenger of the gods, and is often represented wearing a winged hat and boots or sandals.

64. *Venter auribus caret.* See the *Adages* in Erasmus, *Opera omnia*, ed. Jean Le Clerc, vol. 2 (Leiden: Petrus Vander, 1703), col. 659f.

of these ladies[65] will see to it that, although I do not have the voice of Orpheus, I will suffer a similar death. I would like to make peace with them since I consider myself safer among the Furies of Hell than between two infuriated ladies:

Orpheus through his demise	*Orfeo col proprio scempio*
Left a warning for the wise.	*Me n'addita l'esempio.*

He was served by stones, honored by plants, followed by wild animals, admired by monsters, revered by the Furies—he escaped from Tisiphone and Megaera[66] (incredible!)—and was stoned by the women of Thrace.[67] The stones, first animated by his song, in the hands of those women returned to their true, ungratefully cruel nature and put to death the one from whom a little earlier they had received life. And that voice—which silenced the howls of Cerberus and appeased Hell—refused to obey the laws of the Fates and tied together again the thread of a life they had cut off. He canceled the death sentence handed down by the most severe judges of the Shades, he softened the hearts of Minos and Rhadamanthus,[68] yet he hardened the animus of those women. Dying, he left eternal testimony to the world that it is easier to please Hell than the heart of a woman.

Where can I take refuge, if not to flee the hate—that matters little—at least to protect myself from the blows? The laurel trees of Apollo are not safe from these fulminations. Quite the contrary, the laurel, since it was a woman once, to please those of her sex, will offer its branches to make their shafts.

Most Serene Grand Duke,[69] may the altar of your grace offer refuge to my wits and a safe haven for my discourse.

From women's rancor let our wits repair	*Da l'odio de le donne i nostri ingegni*
Beneath your regal laurels in your shade,	*Sotto i tuoi regi allori, O Sol toscano,*
O Tuscan Sun, and let their scorn be spent	*Si ricovrino a l'ombra e spenti siano*
In the sea of your great generosity.	*Nel mar de le tue grazie i loro sdegni.*

THE END

65. Presumably the ladies present at the academy meeting when Buoninsegni delivered his discourse. See Introduction, 13, and note 40.

66. Tisiphone and Megaera are two Furies (also called Erinyes or Eumenides); the third is Alecto. In the Ovidian myth, *Metamorphoses* 10.45–46. Orpheus's sad story made the Furies cry.

67. Buoninsegni recounts the story of Orpheus who, having with his music enchanted the stones and plants, tamed the animals, and moved the Underworld to pity, was in the end the victim of the women of Thrace (in another version the Maenads) who tore him apart.

68. Two judges of the dead in Hades.

69. Ferdinando II de' Medici (1610–1670), Grand Duke of Tuscany (1621–1670), was present at the meeting of the academy when Buoninsegni delivered his discourse.

Antisatire
by Arcangela Tarabotti
in response to
Against the Vanities of Women, a Menippean Satire
by Signor Francesco Buoninsegni

TO THE READER

Never, or rarely, or only with great delay, do the curious writings of today's intellectuals find their way into women's prisons, and so it happened that the *Satire of the Vanities of Women*, written by Signor Francesco Buoninsegni and published some five years ago, has only very recently come into my hands. It was given to me by some gentlewomen who immediately asked me to write a response to it. As a woman inclined and obliged to have other thoughts in my head than to respond to satires or to any profane writing, I refused to do so and objected as strongly as I could; I also resisted, fearing or, rather, knowing I would certainly be derided by men for being five full years late with my response. But so what! In the end I had to give up and satisfy the requests of persons who should and could command me to do it, despite my being greatly mortified. And so, having obtained from these illustrious ladies an almost solemn oath that they would never allow my present composition to come to the attention of anyone of the male sex, I had to cast off any reservations and take courage from that common popular adage, *better late than never.* I feel certain that men, unless they lie, will not be able to say that I am creating a *Vanities of Men,* or a *Countersatire,* out of spiteful vendetta, since I live far from where I might wear high wooden shoes, makeup, and such women's garments as those detested and decried passionately and sincerely by this worthy author. Oh, if only everyone considered those beams they have in their eyes and did not point with contempt and blame to the mote in their brother's.[1] I mean to imply that if this clever fellow were impartial and indifferently sought to examine the superfluous adornments of men as well as those of women, he would not have chosen to make the small errors of one side seem numerous while diminishing the serious excesses of the other. I know, dear reader, that you are kind and endowed with intelligence, I know that you know how to understand, distinguish, refute, and prove, and, therefore, I ask you, if you are a man, not to take it in a bad way if it seemed to you that I have gone too far. Please know that I am about to

1. "And why seeth thou the mote that is in thy brother's eye, and seest not the beam that is in thy own eye?" (Quid autem vides festucam in oculo fratris tui et trabem in oculo tuo non vides?). Matthew 7:3; also in Luke 6:41.

respond as well I should to the attack,[2] even though Divine Law orders the good Christian who has been slapped on one cheek to offer up the cheek that was not offended;[3] in any case it is always a blameworthy action to be the first to offend. If Signor Buoninsegni might feel he has been stung, being the very prudent gentleman he is, he should not take offense, since the provocation comes from him; nor should he ever believe that I speak with rancor to offend him, but it is rather to defend with the truth my sex that has been unfairly insulted by his pen, which is, moreover, quite famous.[4] And I, before responding, kindly ask his pardon, as his esteemed condition merits. The Egyptians wisely designated as a sign of envy the rock partridge, a bird that instinctively, when it drinks from a limpid and clear stream, works as hard as it can with its beak and feet to muddy the water so that other birds are unable to drink there.[5] So too this gentleman, having sated his intellect at the crystalline fountain of the worth of women[6] and, having become acquainted with their pure and forthright qualities, has managed, with the beak of his sharp tongue, biased conceits afoot, to contaminate the pure waters of their prerogatives so that other men might not satisfy their mental thirst by considering such limpid waters.[7] Do not listen to what he has to say, nor believe that I have decided to respond to him motivated by any interest or passion of my own. You know that the command of powerful people can make anything happen. Be assured, moreover, that I have no other complaint against men than the one that swelled up in me when I read in Sacred Scripture that the first words that came

2. Tarabotti uses the expression *sto … sul pontiglio di*, a variation of *sto sul punto di* (to be about to), which substitutes *puntiglio*, meaning "point of honor" or "quibble," for "punto." This play on words suggests not only that the writer is about to write something but also that she is about to participate in a discussion and express a difference of opinion—to take a stand. I've tried to add this meaning with the expression "as well I should."

3. "If one strike thee on thy right cheek, turn to him also the other" (Si quis te percusserit in dextera maxilla tua praebe illi et alteram.) Matthew 5:39.

4. Elsewhere Tarabotti writes: "He who stings must be stung and he who damages another's reputation deserves to have his honor pierced." Tarabotti, *Letters*, 152 (letter 99).

5. The source of this comparison is Pierio Valeriano's *Hieroglyphica*. Tarabotti may have consulted the Italian translation of this text that was published in Venice in 1602 and again in 1625. Valeriano claims that the rock partridge, because of this reprehensible behavior, is the symbol of an evil-natured and envious man. See *Ieroglifici, overo Commentari delle occulte significationi de gli Egittij, & d'altre nationi* (Venice: Gio. Antonio and Giacomo Franceschi, 1602), 364.

6. This would seem to be a reference to Moderata Fonte's profeminist dialogue *The Worth of Women* and evidence of the fame it enjoyed, since Tarabotti assumes that Buoninsegni is familiar with it: *Il merito delle donne … ove chiaramente si scuopre quanto siano elle degne e piú perfette de gli huomini* (Venice: Domenico Imberti, 1600).

7. Like the rock partridge, once Buoninsegni has benefited he makes it difficult for others to do so: just as the rock partridge uses its head and feet to contaminate the water, preventing others from imbibing it, so this author, Tarabotti writes, would keep others from learning about the worth of women.

out of the mouth of the first man, even though he had just been created by the hand of God, were in accusation of a woman.[8] From this event I deduce what one can expect from other men, but regarding the rest of them (the merciful and most just will of God be praised), I am not in a situation in which I frequent them or experience their evil. I have learned many things from my relationships with innumerable women who were betrayed, gravely hurt, neglected, abandoned, and I must say suffocated rather than married. Ancient authors, even though they were men, left us quite vivid examples of this and now, from the mouths of these same unhappy women bound in marriage, my own ears hear complaints and grievances for the cruelty, intimidation, tyranny, impiety, and infidelity of wicked husbands, such that would earn pity in Hell. I promise you then, if my grave indispositions allow me,[9] I will soon build on the foundations of the miseries referred to me by these unhappy women a *Purgatory of unhappily married women*, having already completed *Convent Hell.*[10] If you happen in the meantime to hear complaints about me, defend the justice of my cause, since not only will you be doing what you should, you will be sure to be rewarded by God in Heaven.

8. The accusation that Eve was responsible for the Fall, that it was made first by Adam and then by other men, and the defense of Eve are subjects that Tarabotti treats frequently in her works, for example in Tarabotti, *Paternal Tyranny*, 52; Tarabotti, *Che le donne* (Panizza), 105–106; and Tarabotti, *Letters*, 172 (letter 122).

9. Tarabotti describes her illness as: "A continual constriction of the chest, which consumes me, I might say, to my very bones and nearly takes my breath away, comes over me in the autumn and spring with such vehemence that often it reduces me to a state in which I might suddenly render my soul to my Creator." Tarabotti, *Letters*, 71–72 (letter 17).

10. *Inferno monacale*, written before 1643, was first published in 1990 by Francesca Medioli, who based the text on the only known manuscript, today in the private Giustiniani collection (See Introduction, 9). The *Purgatorio delle malmaritate,* instead, if it ever existed, has been lost.

Antisatire
by A[rcangela] T[arabotti]

Neither Ariosto nor Signor Buoninsegni could have made any better known the guilty conscience they have for vilifying the female sex, as the one does by beginning his mendacious canto and the other his *Satire* against women with those lines,

Ladies, and all who the fair sex esteem,	*Donne, e voi che le donne avete in pregio,*
For God's sake do not listen to this tale.	*Per Dio, non date a quest'istoria orecchia.*

The former puts insulting words in the mouth of a tavern keeper whose mores are those of his less than honorable profession and who was under the influence of wine; the latter confesses that his *Vanities of Women* is an ugly miscarriage produced by his mind, born in a wine-induced ebullience with Bacchus as midwife. One wonders if that great poet and this indefensible enemy of women do not know they deserve to be denounced by everyone, since they ask women themselves—and those who profess to revere them—not to pay attention to their blather. Distancing myself little from their opening, I will say

Ladies and all you who lovers esteem,	*Donne, e voi che gli amanti avete in pregio,*
I ask you please to listen to this tale.	*Date vi prego a questa istoria orecchia.*

I must, however, from the very beginning confess that Signor Buoninsegni is an intelligent person who is as modest as he is learned, since, bringing this work into the world and recognizing it for the miscarriage that it is, he immediately calls it the delirium of an academician, the dream of a sick man, and the complaint of a husband. There is no doubt that in our time most academic discourse deserves the title of madness—not merely delirium. Academicians do not know how to discuss matters of worth without offending that sex that is the glory of the world. The sick only dream of appalling things. How could anything appear more appalling to our minds, or before our eyes, than to hear a man, who received his very life from a woman, denounce her—even reproach her way of dressing—while failing to recognize that such worldly extravagances have grown and spread so much that men too have succeeded in justifying for themselves those vanities that they continuously condemn in the female sex. Thus it is true today that one can freely claim *vanitas est omnis homo.*[11] Dreams, moreover, have for their father Sleep

11. Tarabotti here quotes only part of Psalms 38:6: Ecce mesurabiles posuisti dies meos, / Et substantia mea tanquam nihilum ante te. / Verum tamen universa vanitas, omnis homo vivens (Behold thou hast made my days measurable, and my substance is as nothing before thee. And indeed all things are vanity: every man living). Tarabotti uses *vanitas* to suit her specific purpose here, namely to say that

and their mother Night, from whose darkness Hesiod imagines was born that evil-tongued Momus who has suggested to Signor Buoninsegni these sentiments that argue against the worth of the female sex![12] The complaints of husbands are no more than madness, or rather they are the wicked responses of those who, having deliberately sought and procured a rich dowry, then lament having to provide for the women who made it clear how precious they were by bringing with them so much treasure. If before they had won them in marriage they professed to be their ardent lovers, now they would like for their wives to dress like our first mother so they could more easily waste their money to dress their whores. This is what gives rise to the complaints that so often fill the air in abomination of the dress and pomp of women!

Come now, Signor Francesco, so far we are in agreement. If you will go forward without straying from the truth any more than you have by declaring that your discourse is the delirium of an academician, the dream of a sick man, and the complaint of a husband, instead of earning the reputation of liar and slanderer you will deserve to be known as a just and truthful man. Yet I must add, if you assumed the burden of speaking ill of women but did not ask for it, I am sorry to say that by taking such an action to satisfy others, perhaps even against your own inclination, you show yourself to be an individual of too little conviction.

In this discourse of yours, by calling it the delirium of an academician, you show that you were wise enough to foresee the kind of danger to which you expose yourself. Had it been otherwise, out of prudence you would have refrained from exposing yourself, since you were also aware of the injustice of your rationale, admitting that little or nothing can jeopardize those who have received all the desirable gifts from God and Nature. There is little danger, as I too know, since great and noble souls, like those of women, scoff at, but do not retaliate for the affronts of those who offend them. There is little danger because the female sex is not disdainful, as you assert, but was and always will be most kind and indulgent. Lastly, there is little danger since the malice of men has deprived women of the arms and letters with which they could justly avenge themselves.

---

all of human kind are given over to vanities. She quotes from the same passage in a letter to Girolamo Brusoni: "I declare I am quite familiar with the vanity of worldly glories when I consider the maxim of the wise man, *universa vanitas est omnis homo.*" Tarabotti, *Letters*, 251 (letter 213). In this letter and again in *Paternal Tyranny* her use of the expression is closer to that of the biblical text than it is here: "When you believe you're at the summit of worldly success, you'll realize you are nothing, enjoying nothing but vanities, indeed, becoming one with vanity itself: 'Vanity of vanities is every living man.'" Tarabotti, *Paternal Tyranny*, 78.

12. "And Night bare hateful Doom and black Fate and Death, and she bare Sleep and the tribe of Dreams. And again the goddess murky Night, though she lay with none, bare Blame and painful Woe." Hesiod, *Theogony*, trans. Hugh G. Evelyn-White (Internet Sacred Text Archive, 1914), 211–14 <http://www.sacred-texts.com/cla/hesiod/theogony.htm>. Momus was the Greek god of slander or blame.

Do not, no, mister delirious academician, do not be afraid you will be the victim offered up to the scorn of women, unless you see yourself as the ideal offering to make to the goddess of beauty to whom were usually sacrificed doves. No, do not be afraid, I hasten to repeat, because women, whom you acknowledge to be worthy of adoration, are not looking for a victim, who, calling into question their modesty and goodness, even detests their clothes, which serve their feminine beauty as a veil over sacred things that makes their beauty more decorous and promotes the devotion to it of others.

It is no wonder that Solomon earned the intense scorn of women, having so many of them at his pleasure as are mentioned in Sacred Scripture (*Nonaginta sunt Reginae, et trecentum Concubinae*).[13] They were justly furious, knowing that no one among them could be loved perfectly and they had to let him feel the fulminations of their very righteous indignation.[14] If now you are keen to encounter the ire of women in order to be compared to the wisest of men, be warned that queens will not come from the far corners of the earth just to see you.[15] But, perhaps because you have understood that you cannot be a perfect Solomon, you are content to present yourself as an Achilles who, instead of a warrior's spear, uses language that you claim both wounds and heals at the same time. Wound us as you like, for, as I have said, the strength and resistance of women hold your blows in little account, but beware, for since your tongue is a spear it might be blunted and lose its point when it encounters the adamantine spirit of women, or it may even be repelled and sent back to wound you instead. *Defixerunt linguas suas adversus se ipsos tamquam gladium*, in the words of some evil tongues.[16]

You offer in proof of your opinions that the emissaries of love consider clothing, gold, and jewels to be an excellent way to bring down the bastion of feminine modesty. This is a shameful argument coming from the pen of the secretary of a prince whose splendorous merits make the illustrious glory of the Alexanders, the

13. Ninety queens and three hundred concubines, but see 3 Kings 11:3: Fueruntque ei uxores quasi reginae septigentae, et concubinae trecentae: et averterunt mulieres cor eius (He had seven hundred wives as queens, and three hundred concubines; and the women turned away his heart; 1 Kings 11.3).

14. There is no reference in the biblical text to the scorn of Solomon's wives and concubines. Tarabotti here is responding to the error in Buoninsegni's satire, in which he attributes to Solomon a famous passage from Ecclesiasticus 25:23 on the ire of women: Et non est ira super iram mulieris (And there is no anger above the anger of a woman, Sirach 25:23). See Buoninsegni, *Satire*, 37–38, and notes 4 and 5.

15. As did the Queen of Sheba, who came to Jerusalem to meet the famous King Solomon: 1 Kings, 10:1–3; 3 Kings 10:3 (Vulgate).

16. "They have turned their words upon themselves like a sword." I am unable to identify the source of this quotation or maxim. Tarabotti also uses the expression in a slightly different form: "Linguas suas defixerunt at versus se ipso tamquam gladius." Tarabotti, *Inferno monacale*, 102.

Catos, and Caesars seem abhorrent.[17] The woman who would allow the bearer of amorous emissaries to appear before her, as one of the authors you have cited says,

No woman is, or is a foolish one.	*O non è donna o s'è donna, è sciocca.*[18]

If then she lets herself be persuaded by four silk rags, by pale dregs of the earth, by a piece of hard ice, indeed, by all the treasures that the most valuable mines in India can dispense, not only does she no longer merit the glorious title of woman, but she must be called the scorn and dishonor of womankind. And you, Signor Buoninsegni, are you so—I almost said—audacious that you dare to proffer similar untoward propositions in the presence of most noble ladies?[19] If you managed to escape unscathed, give thanks to that Serene Highness who, since you appealed to him, took you into his protective shade.[20] Yet the indignation of the gods, after a long period of quiet, in the end expresses itself in thunderbolts.

In truth, to support your opinions you marshal texts of philosophy, that is, fantastic tales one tells to the lowest of the common folk.[21] How much, oh how much better you would do if you would exaggerate instead in opposing the betrayals and wickedness of evil men. Rather than disapproving of women's adornments, try using your anger to condemn the diabolic snares set by many men to undermine the honor of women and to revile the modern excesses of men's clothes, now characterized by greater vanity than those of women and far more disgraceful and scandalous. Their fastidious way of dressing is indecorous and unsuitable for men and becomes a sign of a lax and lascivious, indeed vile

17. Buoninsegni was secretary to Leopoldo de' Medici (1617–1675) when the Medici prince was delegated to govern Siena in the absence of his brother Mattias. Leopoldo was a distinguished scholar and patron of the arts; in 1667 he was named cardinal by Pope Clement IX. Tarabotti had initially planned to dedicate the *Antisatira* to Leopoldo before deciding on his sister-in-law, Vittoria della Rovere. See Tarabotti's letter to Pietro Paolo Bissari: Tarabotti, *Letters*, 283 (letter 254).

18. Guarini, *Il pastor fido*, act 1, scene 3, line 631. Taking the line out of context, Tarabotti construes it to convey a meaning entirely contrary to that of Guarini (lines 628–31), who wrote: "A handsome woman sought unto by store / Of gallant youths, if pleas'd with one alone / No woman is, or is a foolish one." Translation by Sir Richard Fanshawe in Guarini, *Il pastor fido*, 89.

19. Buoninsegni addresses women directly several times in his satire, and there were women present at the academy meeting when he delivered his discourse. See the Introduction, 13n40.

20. Buoninsegni's satire concludes with the hope that the Grand Duke of Tuscany, Ferdinando II de' Medici, will offer him protection in the "shade" of his "regal laurels." Buoninsegni, *Satire*, 54.

21. Tarabotti, especially in *Paternal Tyranny*, expresses her disdain for philosophers like Aristotle and his followers who argue for the inferiority of women: "Oh how much more it is with envious spite than with sincere truth that you call woman an imperfect animal" (O con quanto più di livore invidioso, che di verità sincera, dai titolo d'animal imperfetto alla femina). Tarabotti, *Semplicità ingannata*, ed. Bortot, 357. See also *Paternal Tyranny*, 133, and my discussion in Elissa B. Weaver, "'With Truthful Tongue and Faithful Pen': Arcangela Tarabotti against Paternal Tyranny," in *Speaking Truth to Power from Medieval to Modern Italy*, ed. Jo Ann Cavallo and Carlo Lottieri, *Annali d'Italianistica* 34 (2016): 290–91.

and obscene mind. Ancient philosophers and men of times gone by who were truly virtuous had contempt for extravagant display in clothing and adornment. A modern bard writes

But thatched of humble reeds	*Ma di vil canna inteste*
Their houses were, thus Consuls of Rome	*Le case furo, onde con chiome incolte*
With hair unkempt would oft leave home.	*I consoli di Roma uscir piú volte.*[22]

They dedicated themselves to virtuous speculations, to ethics, to living respectably—they were not depraved and effeminate men who spent time attending to their hair and grooming their beards—and yet they conquered and ruled over the world, probably without thinking about such politics and interests of state[23] as today succeed in nauseating Heaven itself.

But let us return to the champion of men who, with a certain use of grammar that I do not understand at all, would infer that *lusso* (luxury, vanities) and *lussuria* (lust) are the same thing; and I do not deny it but, since women's *lusso* is not *rio* (evil), as he says it is, it is not *lussuria.*[24] The *lusso* of men can well be called *rio* and foul, but, since I am not permitted to discuss such things, I will leave it to their consciences to consider the extent to which they have gone with *lusso rio* (evil vanities) such that they deserve to be punished, not only by God and the world, but by the very elements themselves. If they were to imitate the ancients, instead of studying in the mirror how to arrange their hair, they would study how to beautify their souls; nor would they write sophisms and argue paradoxes to disadvantage women, whom they have, through their cunning, kept so far away from an education that when the occasion arises they either do not know how or do not want to defend themselves, and it is then they who seem to be the evil ones, guilty of every fault, and the men the most innocent.

22. The author of these lines is Fulvio Testi (1593–1646). See *Opere di Gabriello Chiabrera e Fulvio Testi* (Milan: Nicolò Bettoni, 1834), 396. I thank Amyrose McCue Gill for this reference.

23. Her criticism of the "interests of state" (as I have translated *ragioni di stato*) is personal, though the term was widely used in the seventeenth century; here it refers to the complicity of the state in the practice of confining daughters to convents even against their will in support of maintaining the social order of the state, a practice Tarabotti criticizes in all of her writing. See, for example, Tarabotti, *Paternal Tyranny,* 60.

24. This ridiculous play on the words in Buoninsegni's satire to which Tarabotti answers is impossible to translate, so I leave the Italian terms—*lusso, rio,* and *lussuria*—and provide English equivalents in parentheses. The term *lusso,* which is in the title of Buoninsegni's satire, while close to the English term *luxury,* is best translated as "vanities" since with it Buoninsegni refers primarily to expensive and extravagant clothes, shoes, and hair styles.

I prefer not to discuss here these most truthful sentiments that I have put forth more thoroughly in my *Paternal Tyranny*,[25] yet I will not fail to respond to the eloquent discourse of one who, assuming the role of reformer of human behavior, says to all the world that in order to make women renounce the vanities it is first necessary to divest them of their ignorance. Oh, what an evangelic pronouncement out of a mouth that is not always truthful! It would be most praiseworthy and of great utility to everyone to engage women in those studies that men cultivate assiduously. Once the dark clouds of ignorance that surround them were dispelled, you would see well, O mister sick dreamer, that women would turn out to be the shining suns, that you, despite the way men are normally inclined to think, are willing to admit they are. It is truly from the splendor of their beauty that the world receives all those benefits that the sun dispenses to mortals on this lowly earth. If they are suns, then their adornments serve as rays of light.

The finest linens, the purest gold, the whitest pearls, and the most precious jewels—and everything else found here below that is most beautiful and excellent—are judged worthy to adorn the vestments of holy priests. One can say that woman is something sacred and belongs to God because of her goodness and piety. *Intercede*, the Church sings, *pro devoto foemineo sexu*.[26] A woman in heaven is the earth's advocate before God: *Eia, ergo advocata nostra*, as even men acknowledge.[27]

Let a woman's beauty then be adorned with the most luminous, beautiful, and precious accoutrements that rich treasuries can buy, if for no other reason than because she is a living and most pure ray of the Divine and because her just and holy actions are exemplary. But today, poor feminine justice and sanctity—or rather, poor women—for all your justice and sanctity you are excluded from every position of honor, from every function in public forums. Ever more greatly maligned, we are held as prisoners,[28] because every day the perfidy of men grows greater, and indeed this situation proves

25. Tarabotti devotes much of the second book of the treatise to advocate for women's education. See Tarabotti, *Paternal Tyranny*, 97–109.

26. "Intercede on behalf of holy women consecrated to God." The reference is to an antiphon used for various feasts of the Virgin Mary: Sancta Maria, succurre miseris, juva pusillanimes, resolve flebiles, ora pro populo, interveni pro clero, intercede pro devoto femineo sexu: sentiant omnes tuum juvamen, quicumque celebrant tuam sanctam festivitatem. See <http://www0.cpdl.org/wiki/index.php/Sancta_Maria,_succurre_miseris>.

27. Tarabotti cites a line of the *Salve regina*, the best known of the four major antiphons recited in honor of the Virgin Mary at the end of the canonical hours. In full: Eia, ergo, advocata nostra, illos tuos misericordes oculos ad nos converte (Turn then, most gracious advocate, / Thine eyes of mercy toward us). See <https://www.catholicnewsagency.com/resources/prayers/marian-prayers/hail-holy-queen>.

28. Tarabotti changes the subject of the verb from "you are" (*sète*), with which she began discussing the injustice to women, to "we are" (*siam*), including herself clearly here in the company of women who are treated unjustly and imprisoned by the "perfidy of men."

That we get worse as we go along,	*Che noi mai sempre peggiorando andiamo,*
Since fathers are not as good as their forebears,	*Poiché degli avi i padri son men buoni,*
And more evil than fathers are their sons.	*E viziosi piú de' padri i figli.*[29]

Oh, evil and perverted mind of men who are unable to write of lofty deeds and tell stories of virtue, since in our time very few men perform actions worthy of immortality! Almost all of them write maliciously to denounce and disparage the noble actions of women, and they expect to become immortal with such works that only show them to be monsters of ingratitude! Just listen to that man who decries women's dress and does not complain zealously that so much attention to dress makes women neglect religious observances, or badly waste their time adorning themselves, nor that some women dangerously risk their honor to make certain fools fall into traps that were not meant for them.[30] Instead he laments that vanity is the enemy of love, and that women busily embellishing their looks have no time for idleness, which is the father of love. Oh, what crass hypocrisy it is to disparage the appearance of evil because it prevents a real and greater evil. Oh, what a laughable satirist! He knows no other way to cry about the harm women cause by attending to their looks than with tears borrowed from his own passion! Bad news, he says, for lovers, that women are kept busy for an entire year arranging elaborate hairstyles—and we do not have time to listen to their fallacious blather.[31]

But let us leave behind these sentiments, however true and harsh, with which we have responded to a worthless argument and turn our attention to deriding men, since it is laughable that they detest the very defects that they themselves exhibit. Is it not because they envy their beauty that many men like monkeys seek to imitate women in every way? We see no one else but Adonises and Narcissuses strolling the streets and profaning our churches. But they should beware of turning into flowers, since there will be no nymphs and goddesses around to celebrate their funerals with sorrow and tears.[32] Oh, how many, how very many young men

29. These lines are taken from Bartolomeo Arnigio, *Le dieci veglie di B. Arnigio degli ammendati costumi dell' humana vita* (Brescia: Francesco e Pietro Maria fratelli de' Marchetti, 1577), 8. I thank Amyrose McCue Gill for this reference.

30. I have rephrased Tarabotti's figure of speech, commonly used in Italian, "to make certain birds fall into nets not meant for them," which might not be easily understood in this context. Tarabotti is responding to Buoninsegni (*Satire*, 38–39, and note 8), who suggests that women use beautiful clothes to attract lovers; she adds here a list of perils which should concern him, the last being that extravagantly dressed women might jeopardize their virtue by unwittingly attracting lovers.

31. See note 28 above. Here once again Tarabotti, by changing the subject from they to we, includes herself among the women disparaged by their critics.

32. The reference is to the nymph Echo and the goddess Venus, who wept at the death of Narcissus and Adonis, their lovers who had metamorphosed into flowers: Narcissus into the homonymous flower

in our time go about excessively groomed, foppish, perfumed, and lewd. I just do not know how men can be so audacious that they detest what they themselves practice without shame and fear of having to hear themselves reproached for it. *Qui praedicas non furandum furaris. Medice cura te ipsum.*[33] Everything that Signor Buoninsegni detests in his criticism of women one sees today explicitly in the actions and customs of men.

How can they say that ostentatious clothes are signs of slavery, punishment for the ancestral sin for which they were to blame? *Per unum hominem peccatum intravit in mundum.*[34] Scripture speaks clearly. You must agree that clothing is evidence of the sin that good women abhor so greatly that it must also be proof of feminine modesty, since our first mother, when she saw that she had lost her innocence through Adam's fault, despising that evil deed, ran immediately to cover herself. I believe it is incontestable that she was the first who *tulit folia ficus, et fecit sibi perizomata.*[35] Clothes, then, on a woman, are a sign and the proof of her modesty and of her willing and necessary hate and loathing of the guilty act; it is not a sign of the sin of which she is most innocent.

Why disparage silk in women's attire because it is the vomit of worms, since women cover themselves with it precisely to have constantly before their eyes an object through which to contemplate the nature of worldly vanities? Is it not the case that you men, worms of the earth that you are, wear not only silks but also gold and diamonds with such indecent lasciviousness that it makes the world and Heaven sick? What woman has ever been found who so exorbitantly dedicated herself to the vanities of bodily adornment as much as that prince of Peru, who was so vain and effeminate that each day, after having daubed himself well all over with a certain perfume, had himself sprinkled thoroughly with powdered gold so that he looked

(Ovid, *Metamorphoses* 3.407–510), Adonis into an anemone (10.519–739).

33. Two biblical quotations which Tarabotti cites together also in *Inferno monacale* (90): Paul, Romans 2:21: "Thou that preachest that men should not steal, stealest"; and Luke 4:23: "Physician, heal thyself."

34. Paul, Romans 5:12: Propterea sicut per unum hominem peccatum in hunc mundum intravit (Wherefore as by one man sin entered the world). Tarabotti cites this passage also in *Paternal Tyranny* (122) at the end of book II, where she adds *et per foeminam gratia* (and through a woman grace). See Tarabotti, *Che le donne siano* (Panizza), 25, where she completes the quotation making it explicit that only Adam and not Eve was responsible: "*per unum hominem peccatum intravit in mundum*, non per due" (through one man sin entered the world, not through two); Tarabotti, *Women Are of the Human Species*, 105.

35. She took fig leaves and made herself aprons. The reference is to Genesis 3:7, a passage which Tarabotti changes from plural to singular (except for *perizomata*, loin coverings, or aprons) to support her claim that it was Eve who first covered her nakedness. The line in Genesis is: Et aperti sunt oculi amborum, cumque cognovissent se esse nudos, consuerunt folia ficus, et fecerunt sibi perizomata (And the eyes of them both were opened: and when they perceived themselves to be naked, they sewed together fig leaves and made themselves aprons).

like a golden statue?[36] This man, this one, turned necessity into pride, need into luxury, and let it be known that, as the heart of a man makes gold his paradise and no other glory worth pursuing, his body is a hell of sins, embellished, ornamented, and polished with that metal for which there is no evil deed he will not commit. And he pretends to be surprised that it can have an effect on a woman's mind!

There are infinite examples of men who are vain, lascivious, who attend assiduously to their hair styles, to makeup, to scents, perfumes, and to all those things condemned in women by our most gentlemanly satirist with such loathing. There is an endless abundance of those of the virile sex who are effeminate, effete, and shameful.[37] Lysicrates paid no less attention to brushing his hair than women today to constructing a wig, and, in changing his hair from white to black, he demonstrated that he too deserved to be mentioned by Ovid as one of the miracles of those gods who transformed men into beasts.[38] Abron never failed to imitate women in his acts and movements as well as hairstyle and cosmetics.[39] What were Strato, Aristodemus, and others not willing to do with effeminate vanity?[40]

What do you make of that, mister censor of women's dress? Would it not be better for you to spend your admirable eloquence to deride men's rather than women's vanity? But all you writers, instead of telling the truth you treat the poor women badly and favor with adulation those of your own sex. And so it is that Maecenas received the praise of every ancient bard, and yet Augustus wrote and criticized him for being too lascivious, utterly vain, and the inventor of immoderately refined appetites; but what was worse about him was that he lived this

36. She refers to the legend of El Dorado, about which Consalvo Ferrando de Oviedo wrote to Cardinal Bembo. The letter was published by Giovanni Battista Ramusio in a work entitled *Navigazione del grandissimo fiume Maragnon*. See Giovanni Battista Ramusio, *Navigazioni e viaggi*, ed. Marica Milanesi (Turin: Einaudi, 1988), 6:869.

37. Tarabotti takes her examples of men who are "effeminate, effete, and shameful" from Ravisius Textor (Jean Tixier de Ravisi), *Officina, sive theatrum historicum et poeticum* .... (Basel: Sumptibus Ludovici Regis, 1617), 5.31 (*De Mollitie ac hominibus effoeminatis*). The *Officina* was also published in Venice in 1617. I thank Paolo Cherchi for this reference.

38. Ravisius Textor, *Officina* 5.31.598: Lysicrates abiit in vulgi fabulam, quod iam senio confectus capillos fucaret, ut speciosius videretur & iuvenis (Lysicrates was widely ridiculed because in his old age he would dye his hair in order to look young and beautiful).

39. Ravisius Textor, *Officina* 5.31.599: Fuit & Abron quispiam vitae adeo corruptae & effoeminatae ut locum pa<r>oemiae sequenti reliquerit: Abronis vitam agens. De molliter ac deliciose viventibus (And there was also a certain Abron who led such a corrupt and effeminate life that he inspired the following saying: "To live like Abron." Said of those who live in luxury and effeminacy).

40. Ravisius Textor, *Officina* 5.31.598: Stratonem Sidonium Theopompus scripsit mortales omnes superasse deliciis & mollicie ... Caelium testis est, Aristodemum tyrannum apud Cumae in Romanis antiquitatibus mollem fuisse cognominatum, quod parum vir esset, ac pudicitiam substravisset (Theopompus wrote that Strato of Sidon surpassed all mortals in luxuries and effeminacy ... Caelius [Rhodiginus] testifies in *Lectiones antiquae* that in Cuma the tyrant Aristodemus was known as effete because he was a weak man and disguised his weakness as modesty).

way until he was old and decrepit. It was written of him: *Maecenas, mel gentium ebur Etruriae, lasar Aretinum, Tiberinum margaritum, Cilenorum smaragde, iaspis Figulorum, berille et carbunculum Porsenae.*[41]

Do not think, Signor Buoninsegni, that because I have gotten a bit off track I have forgotten to respond to you. Because a woman wears silk you say that she is a worm. This is a conclusion unworthy of your most excellent mind and which should earn you the disdain of every lady; but, because I belong to that sex and we are all kind and reasonable, the only punishment I would administer to you would be to invite all the academicians who heard you deliver this speech to suspend for ten years the good opinion they have of you. How is it that women are worms because they wear the sepulcher of a worm? That *is* a good one! The most poisonous worms are all those men who eat away at a woman's honor and who have so consumed her freedom that she is left with nothing. I would to God that women's garments had, as you say, the same effect on men as the one Deianira sent him had on Hercules,[42] then I would advise all women to disrobe and give their clothes freely to their husbands, lovers, or to other men, so that perhaps in the future they would not suffer such tyranny from them, nor would so many women be buried alive.

Those who are blinded by the splendor of the garments their ladies wear, having greater regard for the accidental than for what is substantial,[43] make it clear that they are fools and unworthy of the kind attentions of any woman. For it is not the clothes, nor the corporal beauty, nor the elegance—these things are sought out of lust and not human affection; it is rather the beauty of the soul, genteel conversation, and untainted modesty that should be loved by one who professes to be a true and worthy lover. These qualities, the sign of a beautiful and pure soul, were what Plato praised in his Stella and Petrarch in Laura; indeed Petrarch, seeing beauty and honesty combined in his beloved, exclaimed "O rarest prodigy of

41. Macrobius, *Saturnalia* 2.4.12: *In epistula ad Maecenatem* …: Vale mel gentium meculle, ebur ex Etruria, lasar Arretinum, adamas Supernas, Tiberinum margaritum, Cilniorum smaragde, iaspi figulorum, berulle Porsenae, carbunculum (In a personal letter to Maecenas …: "Farewell, my honey of all the world, … my ivory of Etruria, lasar of Arretium, diamond of the Adriatic, pearl of the Tiber, emerald of the Cilnii, potters' jasper, beryl of Porsenna, carbuncle). See Macrobius, *Saturnalia*, trans. Robert A. Kaster, vol. 1 (Cambridge, MA: Harvard University Press, 2011), 349–51. In this passage the Emperor Augustus ridicules Maecenas imitating his exuberant style. The text was adapted in Tarabotti's source, the same chapter in Ravisius Textor (*Officina* 5.31.599) that she uses for the other men mentioned above (see notes 37–40). Gaius Maecenas (68–8 BCE) was a friend and advisor to Emperor Augustus and an important patron of poets.

42. The cloak Deianira sent to her husband Hercules was soaked with the blood of the centaur Nessus. It burned Hercules so badly that he threw himself on a funeral pyre and died. See Hesiod, *Catalogue of Women*, fragment 25.18–33; Ovid, Heroides 9 (Deianira to Hercules); and Ovid, *Metamorphoses* 9.101–238.

43. Tarabotti adopts the philosophical terminology of Aristotle in which the "accidental" refers to the things that are changeable—that vary—as opposed to the "substantial"—a species or kind considered universal and unvariable.

womanhood!"[44] Their affections were not directed to devious and indecent ends, nor were their beloved ladies left abandoned at their doorstep, because the ardor of both, the lovers and their ladies, was honest and the flames of their love most pure.

To anyone who might ask me if I believe that madrigal "Let every woman take up the arms of scorn for men" (*Contro gli uomini ognuna armi lo sdegno*)[45] came from the pen of a woman, I would ardently declare never to fall for such an erroneous opinion. I firmly believe that it has been invented in order to strengthen reasoning so weak that it needs to find corroboration. Women would certainly know how to create something better with which to oppose men than poorly written madrigals, were it not that men have claimed for themselves a great advantage over women, among whom only very few can dedicate themselves to the noble activity of writing. Because of the tyranny of men they have been held back from even learning to read and denied any access to the light of learning and literature.

Those men who are raised from their tender years in studies of grammar and the humanities (although this they could not even name, being the monsters of cruelty they always have been) later take up the study of rhetoric, logic, philosophy, and other sciences. How perverse a thing it is that if, after sweating over their studies for so long and learning to put a bit of twaddle on paper, they believe and boast that they are glorious inventors of new ways to write! I am not referring here to you, Signor Buoninsegni, since I have learned from trustworthy sources to revere you as a gentleman and scholar, as unpretentious as you are prudent. Those men, I say, who in order to seem the foremost masters of the entire literary world, if they happen to see a woman using a pen instead of a needle, swear on the Bible and invent a thousand objections to her writing, claiming that it cannot be that a woman can write unless she borrows her tiny glimmer from the most perfect light of their brilliant minds. This they claim even though her light gives off rays of truth purer than those of the noontime sun in a pellucid sky. And so it has happened that many evil tongues and ignorant men claim that *Convent Paradise* cannot be the product of my wits or the flight of my pen, or else, if it were so, it must necessarily have been embellished, ornamented, and enriched with elements of philosophy and theology borrowed from men of superior intelligence. I do not know how otherwise to respond if not to appeal to these most judicious and speculative intellects, who brag about their exceptional minds and unhesitatingly affirm the truth of things that are mere conjecture, and ask them to try to find out who was that philosopher, theologian, or whoever had a hand in the embellishment of my

44. An epigram *To Stella* is attributed to Plato. It is, in the translation of Percy Bysshe Shelley: "Thou wert the morning star among the living, / Ere thy fair light had fled; / Now, having died, thou art as Hesperus, giving / New splendour to the dead"; <https://www.poemhunter.com/poem/epigram-i-to-stella>. The line by Petrarch is from the *Canzoniere* (*Rerum vulgarium fragmenta*) 347.5: "Oh de le donne altero e raro mostro." See Francesco Petrarca, *Canzoniere*, trans. John Gordon Nichols (New York: Routledge, 2002).

45. Buoninsegni attributes the madrigal to an unnamed woman writer.

Paradise. If they have done me this favor, I would be happy if they would kindly let me know. Let these great literati croak as much as they like, but let them also know that I take no greater pride in any other merit of my book than that no men have had a hand in it.[46] Moreover, since those close to me went against my wishes and published it, had I known then, as I do now, that in this city there is a publishing house run by women alone, I would not have allowed it to have been printed by men, as I consider most men unworthy to have any part in *Paradise*.[47] Were they not empty-headed and ignorant they would see in my works those shortcomings that there truly are and they would not resort to inventing them in order to suppress that little bit of good reputation that I can expect, if only because of the passion which I have given to it. I am like a raucous cicada whose voice is a screech amidst the harmonious sounds of so many modern sweet-voiced swans who look so benevolently upon my imperfections.[48] They should know that those notions of theology which I have used are not such profound matters that they cannot be understood by all persons of average intelligence, who should not have to go looking for them in their treasure trove of learning; and those philosophical matters are the kind one receives from the light of natural reason alone and not from their splendid erudition, which shows up perhaps nowhere more than it does in their slander. Let them say (if they are aware of it) that I do not write with the requisite art and order—I confess this myself—and that I cite Latin phrases, not because I am well versed in that language, but because a great amount of it remains in my memory from my daily recitation of the Divine Office, which contains a good part of Sacred Scripture. Let them say that what has profited me the most has been the extraordinary pleasure I always take from reading good books, both religious and profane, Latin and vernacular, through which, however crudely, and without anyone to teach me, I have somewhat smoothed out the roughness of my intellect, and that this, together with the natural disposition bestowed on me by His Divine Majesty, has made me more audacious than I should be. But let them croak on and say whatever pleases them most, for I deride their false accusations and I take

46. Tarabotti uses the term "gracchiare" which I translate "to croak" (see also Panizza's translation in Tarabotti, *Paternal Tyranny*, 144)—that is, to make a raucous noise, here the noise of the complaint of men against women.

47. She is most likely referring to the printing house run by Laura Salis, the widow of Giovanni Salis, a printer from the Swiss canton Grisons who had a shop in Venice (Venice, Archivio di Stato, Arti, b. 163 and Riformatori dello Studio di Padova, fol. 369). When interrogated as part of the trial of Francesco Valvasense (ASV, Santo Officio, b. 103), Laura Salis says she is seventy-seven years old, that her printing house is in the parish of San Canziano ai Biri, that she employs only one pressman, and that she and her daughter do the rest of the work. She claims to have learned the printing art from her father Domenico Cavalcalupo. I thank Mario Infelise for this information.

48. By calling herself a *raucous cicada* (*strepitosa cicala*), Tarabotti calls attention to her exceptional female voice. Female cicadas are silent; it is the male that makes a constant chirr, which she calls a *gracchiare* or a croaking noise.

great pride in knowing that the purity of my style is like that of the religious state in which I find myself. If my syntax is not well regulated and the presentation of my arguments does not conform to the rules of rhetoric, I care little, because I follow no other rules in my writing than those of my caprice. Among my words you will not find those hithers and thithers that appear in the work of other modern writers.[49] Yet I admire these good Tuscan words since they conform so well to the nature of men whose person and heart never stay quietly in one place but indeed always go variously hither and thither taking pride that

… in a world so mutable and blind	*Che in questo mondo instabile e leggiero*
'Tis often constancy to change one's mind.	*Costanza è spesso il variar pensiero.*[50]

Nonetheless, these words are of no use to me, since I have chosen to live forever in a place where, in action as well as words, I can cry out against the instability that is just as truly characteristic of men as it is mendaciously attributed by them to women. To conclude, I know and do not deny the extraordinary imperfection of my compositions, rather I am greatly surprised that they are not recognized for what they are by someone who would not then find it so difficult to see that a woman wrote them without the help of a man. But many of you (I am sorry to say) are the opposite of the ancient philosophers, who, without any malice of spirit whatsoever, acknowledged and praised, some the writing of Diotima, others that of Sappho; some men have commended Ginevra Veronese, others Cassandra Fedele, Alcestis and Penelope, and innumerable other women, without presuming such absurdities as those which some pretentious modern intellectuals assert of me.[51] Let them do as they like; we hold as an article of the Christian faith that anyone who does not believe in PARADISE will be condemned to Hell.[52]

49. Tarabotti is allying herself with Renaissance anti-Petrarchists (and demonstrating her familiarity with a Renaissance literary and linguistic debate) who referred to the preciosity and often meaninglessness of the language of Petrarchist poets by citing their use of the words *quinci* and *quindi* (hither and thither). See the famous example of this critique in Pietro Aretino, *Cortigiana* (1534 edition), act 2, scene 11.

50. The lines are from Torquato Tasso, *Gerusalemme liberata* 5.3.7–8, only slightly altered. I cite from the English translation Tasso, *The Liberation of Jerusalem*, trans. Max Wickert (Oxford: Oxford University Press, 2009).

51. This list of famous women, historical and mythical, was probably compiled from the lists in Ravisius Textor, *Officina* 4.12.342–46 (*De mulieribus doctis*) and 5.3.551–53 (*De amore coniugale*). Diotima is the ancient philosopher and teacher of Socrates who is praised by Plato in the *Symposium*; Sappho is the famous poet of Lesbos, born ca. 612 BCE; Ginevra (Nogarola) Veronese and Cassandra Fedele are fifteenth-century Italian humanists known primarily for their Latin letters; Alcestis and Penelope are the exemplary wives of ancient literature: Alcestis in Euripides's tragedy of the same name, Penelope in Homer's *Odyssey*.

52. A reference to her treatise *Paradiso monacale*, which some prominent literary figures and correspondents of Tarabotti, primarily Angelico Aprosio and her brother-in-law Giacomo Pighetti, claimed

But where are you, my Signor Buoninsegni? Forgive me if I had forgotten about you while I railed against the evil tongues of others. It was impolite of me to set you aside, almost as if I did not care about the highly esteemed person that you are for me. You, who are wont to be such a kind though impassioned speaker, condemn the variety of colors in women's clothes without realizing that you expose yourself to derision by seeming not to know that it is its variety that makes the world beautiful; nor do you see that there are examples of famous men and kings who have enjoyed indiscriminately all those vanities that you disparage and detest in us. Croesus, the King of Lydia, would appear so pompously dressed and adorned in such a variety of colors and styles that Solon shamed him to tears, pointing out that the peacock, parrot, and other animals covered in feathers were not dressed much differently than he, but that they were decorously enjoying a gift of nature, while he luxuriated shamefully by resorting to artifice.[53]

I do not deny that it would be more appropriate for a woman to dress always in dark colors, but not so that her lovers direct their gaze exclusively to her face. When she is adorned with fancy clothes whose variety of colors share with her eyes the pleasure of receiving the gaze of others, it is not easy, even with her exceptional modesty, to resist the excessive insolence and debauchery of men. What would the unfortunate woman do if they all struck her directly with their concentrated gaze? That sex that men claim to be most weak would have need of great strength. It is rather the case that the color of our garments should always be black as a sign of the sorrow that oppresses us since we are subjected to the tyranny of men and their shameful whims. Truly, as I must confess, Signor Buoninsegni is a gentleman who sometimes tells the truth, in fact, he even does it more than once, acting quite contrary to the normal inclinations of men. After having asserted truthfully that it would be better for a woman always to dress in clothes that are dark rather than in a variety of colors, he then adds that she was created by God to give solace to men. He perhaps understands that

Woman is man's only true solace,	*La donna a l'uomo è sol vero ristauro,*
Sweet respite, and fitting helpmate.	*Dolce riposo, e opportuna aita.*[54]

could not have been her work alone, and for which she must have had help writing from some man. See Tarabotti, *Letters*, 73–74, 105–106, 153, 236, 280 (letters 17, 51, 99, 194, 252).

53. Plutarch's *Lives* (chapter 27, the *Life of Solon*) recount a meeting between Croesus, the King of Lydia, and Solon in which Solon expresses his disapproval of Croesus' extravagant clothes and jewelry. Here, however, Tarabotti perhaps has in mind another version of the anecdote since she adds an admonishment that is not in Plutarch, comparing Croesus's excessive, unnatural attire to the natural raiment of beautiful birds and other animals.

54. These lines are from Bartolomeo Arnigio's *Le dieci veglie* (1577), 51–52. Again I must thank Amyrose McCue Gill for her excellent sleuth work.

I do not believe, however, that he is aware of just what great praise for my sex is in this proposition of his. It is very true, undeniable, that in women there is a great measure of divinity, while the power to provide respite to one who labors belongs to God alone. And so it is that if you are born to travail,[55] they, by divine disposition, are born to offer you solace and restore your spirits.

If then, as though upon a moveable throne, women continually raise themselves up onto a piece of wood that they adorn with the tapestry of their dresses, it is so because, given their worth, they are not allowed to go about on foot like animals. You men, who were made from the dirt of the earth, are for your mortification destined to walk on it. If women with their thoughts are always uplifted from earth and reach out to the heavens, it is no wonder then that like sacred images they are placed on pedestals covered with very precious drapery. You will never find great and magnificent things placed on the ground, but rather they are displayed on high to be looked upon with awe and reverence.

One might also say that a woman should in every respect be held high above the ordinary low things of the earth precisely as a miracle of nature. Since man was formed out of earth and woman from one of his ribs, it stands to reason that she carry herself as high on her platform shoes as the distance from man's foot to his ribs. God and nature created her with this privilege.[56] Moreover, if we consider that ladies' wooden platform shoes are the accidental cause of the length of women's dresses, and that those long dresses make women a living portrait of modesty, we may reasonably say that the shoes are a most modest and praiseworthy invention.[57]

At the sacrifice of the mass and at every other religious function, priests cover themselves with long gowns, as all religious do, and as in ancient times the high priests of the Temple did, no differently from Christians or pagans. Heaven would not allow its ministers to wear those short garments, dress that conveys the insolence and impurity of men. From this it follows that, unless you wish to show little affection for women, you cannot deny that because of their very nature they should wear the rich mantle of religion, piety, and goodness, since in the clothes they wear women imitate priests who most fervently and devoutly offer sacrifices, vows, and prayers to His Divine Majesty.

What will this perspicacious intellectual say about these feelings I express? Will he perhaps deride them or take offense? If he derides them, I will respond by deriding his derisions, and if he is offended by them I am no more bothered by

55. Homo nascitur ad laborem, Job 5:7, seems to be source of this turn of the phrase.

56. That Adam was made out of dirt and Eve of human flesh is one of the arguments for the superiority of women found in treatises belonging to the *Defensio mulierum* tradition. See Boccaccio, *De mulieribus claris* 1.2 and, for example, Galeazzo Flavio Capra, *Della eccellenza e dignità delle donne* (1525), ed. Maria Luisa Doglio (Rome: Bulzoni Editori, 1988), 95.

57. On women's wooden platform shoes see Buoninsegni, *Satire*, note 20 and figs. 5, 6, and 7.

his taking offense than he is by the anger of the entire host of women that he has jokingly mocked, claiming to be afraid of their wooden shoes. He says he cannot be sure he is not about to sink like a ship, not between Scylla and Charybdis,

But between two cliffs of wood	*Ma nel mar de lo sdegno*
In this scorn-filled sea.	*Fra due scogli di legno.*

If he does not fear the scorn of women because they are amiable, I more courageously declare that I do not fear that of men, even though I know they are most cruel.

No, they do not need to have their ears opened up, those ladies who have chosen to keep them held open with very elegant long earrings, the better to hear the voices of preachers and things that concern the eternal salvation of their souls. They do so hoping to one day leave behind the ill treatment they suffer innocently here below on earth and receive the welcome they deserve from the angels up in Heaven.

But here I realize that I am speaking out too seriously against an ingenious wit who perhaps more in jest than truthfully reproaches the female sex.

Put yourself forward to the test, sir, and then you can judge for yourself if it is true that women have more strength in their legs to drag along their high wooden shoes than in their arms to throw them at your head. It is not good to affirm without experience what can be easily demonstrated anytime. You are quite right to be afraid that women might metamorphose into trees, since you fear their arms would then become exceptionally strong. If for them we would need a new Ovid, for men it would suffice to bring back a Lucian or a Lucius Apuleius,[58] but, if that cannot be, women would offer you that very Ovid you would call back for them, since he has shown that he knew how to transform more men than women. Let Actaeon speak, who was transformed into a deer for a sin different from that of the nymph Dryope.[59] Let Battus speak, who was changed into a touchstone for not knowing how to keep quiet and not having kept a promise;[60] and let Tereus speak, the king of Thrace transformed into a hoopoe.[61]

58. Tarabotti suggests bringing back authors who in their works transformed men into animals: Apuleius (ca. 124–170 CE), his Lucius, in *The Golden Ass* and Lucian, presumably Lucian of Samosata (ca. 125–after 180 CE), author of what is thought to be the first example of science fiction, *The True History*, and whose works are filled with fantastic creatures.

59. Ovid, *Metamorphoses* 3.174–252, esp. 186–97: Actaeon is transformed into a deer for having looked at the goddess Diana while she bathed. Tarabotti mentions Dryope (9. 324–93, esp. 349–55) since Buoninsegni cites her example. The nymph Dryope is changed into a lotus for having picked the fruit of the tree into which the nymph Lotis had been transformed.

60. Ovid, *Metamorphoses* 2.687–707: Battus is changed into a touchstone for not having kept a promise made to Mercury not to reveal that he had seen the god with stolen cattle.

61. Ovid, *Metamorphoses* 6.422–674: Tereus, the husband of Procne, is transformed into a hoopoe (lines 673–74) for having raped her sister Philomela and cut out her tongue so she could not tell anyone.

What is especially important to my argument on this subject is that most of the women who underwent transformation were not transformed because of sins they had committed but so they could escape unharmed from the libidinous hands of either gods or men, whose transformations instead all took place in punishment of serious transgressions. But even if you do not have Ovid, you would not fail to transform yourselves on your own, since short though you are, you know how to make yourselves appear tall by putting under the bottom of your shoes a footstool so high that it forces you to walk on the tip of your toes, looking like so many shod horses. Nor are you embarrassed that you make your legs seem good and stout by doubling their size with cotton wool batting (fig. 9). Perhaps, O you scoundrels, it is because you do not think you have lied enough with words that you want to lie as well in deeds and in your appearance—and to do so as lasciviously as possible you spare yourselves no expense, artifice, or trickery. All this just to vie with those ladies, the cut and ornament of whose clothes you impugn, though they are proper and conform naturally to their sex.

If you could bring yourself to be truthful, you would not joke so liberally, making fun of women for their wigs and citing the example of Corisca's Satyr, when many men—many—today transgress wearing abundant hair for which they have paid real cash.[62] It hardly matters if women's hair does not belong to the natural world, but it should not be of little importance that men's hair does not. In these days men are so dedicated to vanities and effete adornments—in particular of their heads of hair, curled with artistry, perfumed, and powdered in the French style—that they see themselves as so many Absaloms.[63] Were they to get hung up in some tree, they would unfortunately remain alive, leaving (and I almost said despite Heaven) their poor innocent tresses stuck there in their stead. Do not boast, no, effete, worthless men, about that bleached and curled hair of yours, which to your shame and for someone's profit was stolen for you from the cadaver of some beautiful woman. If the strength of Samson lay in hair that was naturally his, the same cannot be said of you because in you there can only be cowardice and lack of strength and wit in the same degree as that of the Nazarene when, with the loss of the treasure of his hair for which he was universally admired, he lost all his strength and courage.[64]

62. The example of Corsica's Satyr is taken from Guarini, *Il pastor fido*, act 2, scene 6; see Buoninsegni, *Satire*, 46n30. Tarabotti doesn't argue with Buoninsegni's criticism of women's wigs; she simply responds by accusing men of wearing them too, and very expensive ones.

63. Absalom, the son of David and Maacah (2 Samuel 3:3), was very handsome; he was known for his abundant and beautiful long hair, which eventually was the cause of his death: his hair got caught in the branches of a tree as he sought to escape the army of David, and he was killed: 2 Samuel 14:25–26 and 18:9–15.

64. Judges 16:17–19.

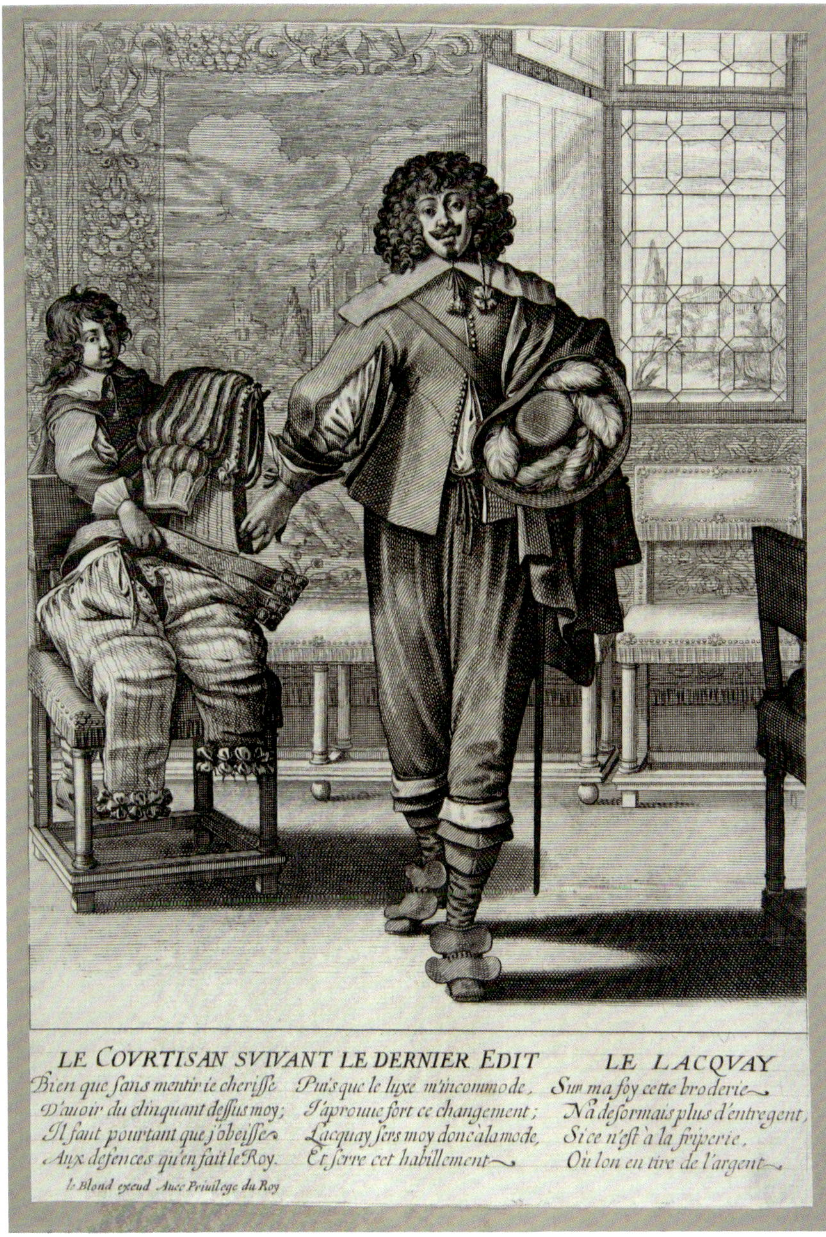

Figure 9. Abraham Bosse, *Le courtisan suivant le dernier édit*, a gentleman renouncing his extravagant clothes that include pants stuffed with batting. Metropolitan Museum of Art, New York, www.metmusuem.org.

Among the host of men, every one of them imagines himself to be a new Aristotle, but instead of seeking to imitate the wisdom that made him immortal, they can take pride only in holding the vain opinions that even that great philosopher held, since they do not imitate his other characteristics.[65] They go about all day inventing contrived arguments to counter the worth of women in order to flaunt their sublime intelligence. Some authors, however, have justly praised their worth, the cause lying more with the heavens than in their own choosing. Listen to the words of an excellent intellectual of our times who attests truthfully and seriously to what Signor Buoninsegni says in irony and jest about the ivory chin and every other part of a beautiful woman:

I will say much less	*Io dirò molto meno*
than what I should, yet I will show	*di quel che dir conviensi, ancor ch’io mostri*
that woman is a noble gift from Heaven:	*che la donna del Ciel sia nobil dono:*
and it is little to call her	*e sia poco il chiamarla*
a treasure of Nature, and little to say	*tesoro di natura, e poco il dire*
that her hair is flaming gold,	*che d’oro il crin fiammeggi,*
her breast shines in a silver light,	*d’argento il sen biancheggi,*
her hand seems ivory, her brow ebony;	*sembri avorio la mano, ebano il ciglio,*
that her eyes are sapphires, her cheeks roses,	*che sian gli occhi zafiri, ostro le guancie,*
her lips coral and her teeth pearls,	*corallo il labro e margarita il dente,*
her eyes are stars and her face is Paradise.	*le luci stelle e Paradiso il volto.*
Little too, if gazing firmly on her one sees	*Poco sarà, se in lei stretto si mira*
nearly all of Heaven displayed	*quasi in compendio il Cielo,*
if in her Nature unfolds all its pomp.	*se in lei spiega natura ogni sua pompa.*[66]

Now what do you say, O you who invent ways to denigrate women? I am speaking generally of all those who write, have written, and will write against the most noble female sex. Truly, reason teaches us that the words of praise that members of the male sex offer to women are much more truthful and laudable than the praise you men go about in turn handing out to one another.

65. The vain opinion of Aristotle to which Tarabotti refers here is his claim in the *Generation of Animals* and elsewhere that woman is an imperfect animal, less fully developed than man and necessarily subject to him. She treats the subject more extensively in *Paternal Tyranny,* where she also includes a brilliant parody of the argument. See note 21 above.

66. These lines, by an unknown author, present the conventional description of feminine beauty—an Italian Renaissance literary commonplace. See, for example, the famous sonnet of Pietro Bembo (1470–1547), “Crin d’oro crespo e d’ambra tersa e pura” (Curls of gold and of pure, lustrous amber).

What a marvel it is that we hear nothing but the denigration of women, on the authority of philosophers, jurists, orators, and poets, and even through purposeful misreadings of Holy Scripture,[67] if almost all those who write and have written are men! Oh, if only women were not forbidden to dedicate themselves to learning and were allowed to study half or a third as much as some men, we would certainly hear ideas that were not contrived or borrowed but rather well-founded and truthful, which would make the male sex blush with shame. Perhaps those of the male sex would not go about so proudly and imperiously speaking ill of womankind, the fount of all human joy.

One of these men is Signor Buoninsegni, who, wanting to suggest a comparison between the Colossus (he says) of Nebuchadnezzar and a woman, expresses his idea with distortions unworthy of the great writer that he is. He turns her upside down and then claims that her head is wooden, unaware that the statue that he mentions has no extremity made of wood: rather, its head was made of gold and its feet of earth. So it is with one who would invent paradoxes and speak ill of another who does not deserve it, he may make others take him for the kind of intellectual who cannot tell the difference between earth and wood. And why did you not say that the beautiful and marvelous structure of a woman raised up on a golden pedestal resembles the most beautiful Colossus of the Sun?[68] Do you know why? Because you belong to that sex, some of whom, rather than telling the truth and speaking positively, choose to tell lies and to speak, as we say, off kilter.

But now it is that, having realized you have spoken rather inappropriately, you want to correct the error and you do so by offering a very good and truthful proposition, saying that a husband is a wooden head to his wife. To his wife a husband is indeed a wooden head and it is not made of strong wood, as we might say of oak or of something similar, but instead it is of the lightest weight, the most fragile, and the most useless wood one can find, hardly good enough to feed a fire. What this flimsy plant produces, with his vain and indecent, affected dress and excessive lewdness, is a call for his wife to imitate him; but the natural modesty of women intervenes and rescues her from the behavior that her husband's bad example might otherwise occasion. This head for his part does not fail to try to arouse impure thoughts in the woman that His Divine Majesty has given him to be his sweet companion, with little fear of God and no regard for self-esteem and with wantonness not unlike that of the Turks, given over to every illicit pleasure.

67. Tarabotti here is referring to the anonymous 1595 treatise entitled *Disputatio nova contra mulieres, qua probatur eas homines non esse* (A new disputation against women, that proves that they are not human), attributed to the German Valens Acidalius, whose argument is based on a continuous misinterpretation of biblical passages. The text circulated in Italy in a translation attributed to Horatio Plata, most likely the pseudonym of Giovanni Francesco Loredan, to which Tarabotti in 1651 published a response, *Women Are of the Human Species*. See Introduction, 10–12, and note 31.

68. A reference to the Colossus of Rhodes, one of antiquity's Seven Wonders of the World, which was seventy cubits high (more than thirty meters).

She, however, does not fail to enclose herself within the gates of an unblemished honesty, as one who was born a sex whose true and proper character is modesty. And men, in imitation of greedy Judas, decide that those four coins used to dress their wives are ill spent, because they consider it better to reserve them for buying other affections. This is like complaining that the ointment with which the Magdalene anointed the feet of Christ is not for sale and using the money to buy something else. Oh, what detestable crimes, oh, what sick minds!

Did I not say a short while ago that, since almost all writers are men, it would always be women who are criticized and who are oppressed by their ideas, which for us, however, seem not to be trustworthy at all, indeed not even in your estimation, if you wanted to tell the truth. You, however, are the sort who would rather die with a sullied conscience than confess the truth, even though you know it very well.

This gentleman decides that he hates it that some ladies wear gold and silver platform shoes, and he immediately comes to the fight with a couplet by Martial that targets a Roman lady who wanted to take advantage of those riches that heaven had given her. Martial was a man and that is enough said. He was as evil-tongued as any other, and he was an enemy of the female sex. As for those who denounce the members of my sex, I feel no obligation whatsoever to trust not just Martial but neither Plato nor Aristotle, unless they first cease to be men. They have cleverly and undeservedly gained great authority in the minds of other men, who as interested parties subscribe to what they say. And they learn to speak ill of women so exquisitely that, as I said above, if some one of us, despite those misguided intellectuals, has a great enough gift from God that she can proudly demonstrate on paper the treasures of an elevated and lively mind (I do not say this about myself), they proclaim with venom and malice that it is impossible that without their help a woman could write with a good natural style and wit. It is as though God might have been partial in giving a greater portion of rationality to men than to women. I laugh at such obvious slander and lies, as I am often reminded of those lines against men that Orsino sang to accuse an evil man:[69]

It will come, the prescribed hour cannot delay,	*Verrà, non può tardar l'ora prescritta,*

69. Tarabotti cites two tercets of a sonnet written by Cesare Orsini entitled "Huomo malvagio" (incipit: "Se l'opre scelerate, e i fatti indegni"), published in his *Diporti poetici* (Venice, Evangelista Deuchino, 1630), 129. In the second line, Tarabotti has omitted the rhyme word "virile" (virile) to suggest a possible rhyme "femminile" (feminine). Since I have not respected the rhyme scheme in my English translation there was no way to reproduce her suggestion other than to fill in the word "woman" in English. Cesare Orsini (1572–still active in 1636) was born in the Lunigiana but spent many years of his life in Venice. Tarabotti may have met him or simply read his poetry through her connection with Giovan Francesco Loredan with whom he associated. For his life and works see Franco Pignatti, "Cesare Orsini," in *Dizionario biografico degli italiani,* 79 (2013): 629–32.

when, thanks to Heaven, the hand of a [woman]	*che sia, mercé del Ciel, da man ...*
will pierce with steel and slash your evil remains.	*l'empia tua spoglia lacera e traffitta*
Meanwhile with my words I will take up the sword	*di ferro, invece intanto io col mio stile*
and press and wound with invincible force,	*premerò, ferirò con forza invitta*
your infamous fame and unworthy, vile name.	*tua fama infame, e 'l nome indegno e vile.*

And, sir, for now, if indeed you speak in jest, you need not worry that your memory fails you, because, if you are happy to give the impression that you are without intelligence for being unwilling to acknowledge the worth of women, you must attribute little importance to the other two powers of the mind.[70] Women are statues with golden feet because they wear gilded platform shoes. Is this not true? If we can deduce the value of a structure from its precious base, what then can we say of the value of the rest of women's bodies if their most base and ignoble part is made of gold? Oh, if this were so, my dear academician, how many, oh how many men would rush to prostrate themselves at women's feet—more, however, out of greed than respect!

Keep your distance from these mobile statues, unless you want them to lose that decorum which statues should never lack, raised up as they are to be admired or adored by everyone. Stay far, far away, you profane men, from the female statues, since as soon as a man approaches them dishonor and danger are at hand. Let a woman keep her distance from a man and, even if she is tainted by the stain of a thousand sins, she will always be honored and considered most pure and innocent. Let her be near to this sordid monster and you see her dishonored, her modesty blemished, her name defamed! And by whom? By that man who is the cause of such hurt and who lacks the inclination and discretion to remain silent and to understand that his reproaches cause her harm. If it does not suffice to calm the passion of others that I concede that we are statues, I will concede yet more, that we are leafless trees, and, if we are without leaves we are not, however, without the fruit of good works. If we are without leaves that are fragile and light, we are not, however, without pleasing and restorative shade.

Woe to you, I say, wicked men, were you to be without the protective shade of feminine truth, goodness, and holiness to save you from the scourge of Heaven.

70. That is, to memory and will as well. The three powers of the mind are intelligence, memory, and will according to Augustine, *De trinitate* 10.11.18: "Memoria, intelligentia, voluntas [sunt] una mens." See also Dante, *Purgatorio* 25.83. Tarabotti's reference about Buoninsegni's memory loss refers to his facetious claim that he cannot remember the entire passage he cites from Martial and so leaves out the off-color expression about the Roman lady's golden chamber pot. See Buoninsegni, *Satire*, 47, and note 38.

An eminent poet of our times,[71] who because he was a man had great difficulty in speaking the truth, in the end was so greatly tormented by his conscience with remorse that he acted against his very nature and said:

Speak, my tongue, speak and say	*Dillo, mia lingua, dillo,*
That woman is, quite rightfully,	*Ch'a ragion è la donna,*
When faith and piety are bound in her,	*Quando fede e pietade in lei si serra,*
Beloved in Heaven and adored on earth.	*Diletta al Cielo e adorata in terra.*

I do not wish to take it upon myself to respond to that story of the husband and the housemaid, because I would have quite a lot to say. God knows what the gentleman had in mind when he called to that servant! Poor gentlewomen, you are made to undergo a strange metamorphosis: mistresses of the house, you often become servants! You are not the Hydra of Hercules, yet in your homes your husbands make you experience the miracle of the Hydra's heads. If out of jealousy you throw a young lady out of your house, they bring on a thousand other women to let you know that they are chameleons who appear in the colors of as many infatuations as there are different faces to gaze upon. They cry about the price they get for grain they must sell to adorn you with those jewels whose value will never diminish and which can serve them should a necessity arise. Then to buy detestable and dishonorable loves they will liberally squander treasures without which they will remain forever exposed and impoverished, and all this besides the harm that will come to their souls and their honor.

Cato had every right to believe that the loss of Roman liberty was at hand when he heard that a fish brought the same price as an ox, but spending on the adornments of one's wife is different from spending to satisfy one's gluttony. You have different ends in mind when you detest the extravagances of women. He desired to see the freedom of the Roman people conserved, and you undermine the freedom of women. That great father of the country would not view without disdain the tyranny used today to imprison women.[72] So it is that the authority of Cato this time, Signor Buoninsegni, turns against you, as does your witty remark about pearls and salt.

71. The poet is Pier Francesco Minozzi (1611–1672) of Monte San Savino. Angelico Aprosio attributes these lines to him in his *Maschera scoperta* (166–67) where he explains that Tarabotti quotes them in her *Antisatira*. On Minozzi's life and works, see Girolamo Ghilini, *Teatro d'huomini letterati* (Venice: Guerigli, 1647), 364–66.

72. Buoninsegni uses the example of Cato the Censor (234–149 BCE) to denounce the disproportionate expense incurred to purchase the jewels used in women's hair styles. Tarabotti here makes it a reference, instead, to Cato Uticensis (95–46 BCE), the symbol of Roman liberty, in order to return to the theme that is most important to her: that of forced monachization, an abuse of power that deprives women of free will.

Truly a man of subtle wit like you does not lack pedantries and sophistries to give vent to your desires and vaunt your worth on the page, *Dulcis est homini panis mendacij*, said the great sage.[73] It is quite a stretch to say, as you have, that pearls and salt are daughters of the sea and that he who lacks salt puts on pearls.[74] These are laughable things—sophisms and veiled lies, not truths. You know this very well yourself. Since the pearl is the most precious, the purest jewel of the most dazzling whiteness, why not say rather that a woman adorns herself with them in proportion to the candor and purity of her soul and of her most divine qualities? I will, however, go along with your conceit, and say that men, because they profess to have the salt (of wit) and yet are without the pearl (of candor), have neither pearls nor salt.

The next conceit, however, that the head of a woman is like a deck of cards, is no less outlandish and bizarre than the previous one. If you refer to her real, physical head, this is just a clever invention of yours meant to make your friends laugh, but if you mean her mystical head and refer to her husband with this term, I accept your opinion as most true and proper.

Most husbands are decks of cards, since they devote themselves to card games, attend to nothing else, think of nothing else, and so, because they continually think only of cards, one may say that their heads have become a deck of cards. Here coins are not lacking,[75] if not true ones at least those coined by a most ardent desire to possess them that strikes repeatedly and for which many men resort to such dishonorable actions that they would sell at the lowest price even the life and blood of another. No one will deny that on these same men, as low and cowardly as they are, we see swords at the ready, if only used to ornament their bodies. Some of them want an excellent, gilded sword to vie with Orlando's, without bearing in mind that they have the heart and arm of the coward Martano to wield it.[76] Not only their servants but the very wives of these valorous knights can testify that they do not lack clubs. In their reckless behavior it is not enough to beat their servants: they use their clubs on her as well whom God has given them as a companion and *adiutorium simile sibi*,[77] that is, not as his inferior and subject

73. Proverbs 20:17: Suavis est homini panis mendacii, / Et postea implebitur os eius calculo (The bread of lying is sweet to a man: but afterwards his mouth shall be filled with gravel).

74. Buoninsegni actually wrote that salt and pearls are "figli"—sons or, generally, children—and not "figlie," daughters, as Tarabotti writes.

75. Coins (*denari*), swords (*spade*), clubs or batons (*bastoni*), and cups (*coppe*) are four suits in a deck of Latin-suited cards (Italian and Spanish) that serve, in this passage (as they do in Buoninsegni's satire) in a series of double entendres.

76. This comparison is with the invincible sword Durlindana that belonged to Orlando, the hero of Italian epic-chivalric poetry, especially of the *Orlando innamorato* of Matteo Maria Boiardo and the *Orlando furioso* of Ludovico Ariosto. Martano in the *Orlando furioso* is a vile and disloyal coward who in a tournament runs away from his adversary.

77. Genesis 2:18: "a help like unto himself," a passage cited also in Tarabotti, *Paternal Tyranny*, 46.

but as an equal, and we might say his superior. Let Bacchus himself be the one to say if this head of a woman that is a deck of cards abounds in cups! This head by emptying many cups fills himself sometimes with so much light-headedness that if he were their real head, as he is their imaginary one, the miserable wives would feel the heavy effect of wine every day.

If you want to see in these cards the faces of Tarots (and this would be to follow in the footsteps of Signor Buoninsegni), look up at the faces of some men and you will see pictured the Devil, the Hanged Man, the Juggler, and the Fool. In many of them the face of Love will appear, but a love that belongs to Tarots—painted, that is, feigned and unreal; with this and with ulterior motives they sometimes hang around women, confusing them in a sea of lies and vowing their passionate love, swearing that their lady's every hair is enough to bind a heart fast and forever, a conceit borrowed from the *Song of Songs: In uno crine colli tui vulnerasti cor meum.*[78] But after these flattering fictions they seem to think they are making a sacrifice to Jove: every time they speak, write, or act, they condemn, malign, and mistreat those ladies, who they had just sworn were the souls of their souls.

And so it happens that we read satires which, instead of detesting these abominable customs of men, curse the expenses that husbands incur for their wives, whose generous dowries—valuable and rich—not only have given their husbands enough revenue for such expenses but also have raised their houses out of poverty and misfortune. With the dowries of their souls women have fostered the happy tranquility and contentment of those who only know how to repay so much good by spreading bad feelings toward those whom they should, so to speak, worship. Do you understand this, Signor Buoninsegni? And you dare to speak of these wives with so little respect. I am astonished by you since everyone praises your admirable courtesy, and I include myself in that expression of esteem.

O foolish men (I am speaking to evil men), senselessly unaware of your best interests, since I have made you see how you are like a deck of cards, why do you not use the coins for the necessary expenses of your families and the appropriate adornment of your wives, the swords to defend your honor and country, the clubs to aid not to harm others, and the cups to give drink to the thirsty, as you are commanded by the Church? Then we would not see in you the horrid faces of the Devil and the others I have mentioned.

Women and flies were not allowed to attend sacrifices in the Temple of Hercules, yet one cannot derive from this the mendacious and contrived conclusion that there is little difference between flies and women. Women have in common with flies only that they are persecuted by all men. So it can be said

78. Song of Solomon 4:9: Vulnerasti cor meum soror mea / sponsa vulnerasti cor meum / in uno oculorum tuorum / et in uno crine colli tui (Thou hast wounded my heart, my sister, my spouse, thou hast wounded my heart with one of thy eyes, and with one hair of thy neck).

of your kind that by reproaching women you are foolishly chasing flies and, in the end, you will have gotten nothing but your hands full of flies. One must in truth affirm that flies, as you say, did not enter the temple out of their natural instinct, and women were excluded because of their beauty. Hercules understood that devotion to him might diminish because their beauty would bring back the shameful memory of the weakness that demigod showed when, having defeated all the monsters of the world, he allowed himself to be defeated by a woman's face and was not ashamed to exchange his club for a distaff and to sit down to spin among the handmaidens of Iole.[79] Or else it was because he feared that the rays of divinity that shine forth from the faces of women would attract those present in the temple and, because of their divine looks and merit, usurp the adoration owed to him; and for this reason he did not want present at the sacrifices those whose divine qualities could compete with his, and women had made it clear that in this they surpassed him.

Let it be though, as you prefer, that the true reason is that the women of Chios, because they refused to pull out their hair so it could be used to bring the image of Alcides[80] into port on the island, were from that time on excluded from attending his sacrifices; and it confers the highest praise on women when the gods themselves demonstrate a great desire to be transported as prisoners of the female sex. If the women did not allow it, it was not in order to maintain their beauty with an impious act, nor because they valued a hair of their head more than a god, but because they did not want anyone to think they would willingly rush to bring in the statue of a hero who had shown himself at times to be lascivious and shameless. Thus they removed the occasion for the evil tongues of the time to damage their reputation. Had the statue been that of the most chaste goddesses Pallas or Diana, they would not only have employed the hair of their heads to bring it into the island but even the blood of their veins. If today the idol of Hercules wanted to land on some shore and women were unwilling to loan it their hair, there would be plenty of lines made from the tresses of men so effeminate that even a god might be tricked into believing it was women's hair. Women in ancient times refused to offer their hair to pull a ship containing the statue of a false god into the port of Chios, and you today, rather than do without that long hair of

79. Hercules fell in love with Iole, the daughter of Eurytus, King of Oechalia, but Tarabotti seems here to remember instead his love affair with the queen Omphale, with whom he exchanged clothes, wore women's attire and jewelry, and in order to stay with her did women's work. Tarabotti's source (but perhaps an indirect one, since she confuses Iole and Omphale) seems to be Ovid's *Heroides* 9, the letter from Deianira to Hercules. In the letter Deianira also recounts the story of the cloak she was given by the centaur Nessus for Hercules to make him forget Iole. It was a trick and caused the hero's death. See Ovid, *Heroides* 9.143–48, 159–64; and note 42 above.

80. Another name by which Hercules was known.

yours, the cause of a thousand mortal sins, refuse to introduce into your soul the true God of all the gods.[81]

You, however, could not say as Charillus did that your hair is your own ornament which costs you nothing, since one of these modern wigs costs no less than five or six ducats. O shameful times, O dishonorable men, who today to festoon their faces all around with a few tufts of curled hair think nothing of spending the money that could raise some poor wretch out of poverty for half a year or which could be invested in charitable institutions for the good of their souls, engulfed as they are in a thousand vices and sins! At least if women buy gowns and jewels to adorn themselves, one may say that they change gold into gold, or into jewels, but you madmen throw gold around to buy what is left on the heads of the dead and the rotten remains in tombs.

It befits a woman to make herself beautiful and you to have fortitude, but you mix up the terms of these expectations, even of nature itself, and you neglect the adornments of the soul; nor is it enough for you to appropriate to yourselves the fashion excesses of women, but you even go on to accuse them of being too pompously ornate and vain, as though you are all like Cato, extremely modest and severe.[82] As I said earlier, the heroes of antiquity did not act this way, and in the words of a contemporary writer:

Phaedra flees with Theseus, and yet unkempt	*Fugge con Teseo Fedra, e pur incolto*
Was his hair, his face hardly clean.	*Egli ebbe il crine, e mal polito il volto.*[83]

In our times, precisely these men who pass themselves off as heroes spare no pomp, vanity, or wantonness that they do not express in the cut or in the lavishness of their clothes—and, what is worse, some of them do so devoting excessive care to their face and their hair style. They have so altered the natural shape of their moustaches that instead of falling over their lips to obstruct their obscene masculine speech they are constrained by iron and fire to raise themselves up menacingly toward the sky.[84] And how then can men harbor such fire in their hearts to detest and denounce the vanities of women?

81. Tarabotti denounces the male fashion of wearing long hair or voluminous wigs as being the occasion of sin, for she sees them as a sign of male effeminacy and relaxed morals.

82. The reference is to Marcus Porcius Cato (234–149 BCE), known as Cato the Censor. See note 72 above and Buoninsegni, *Satire*, note 45.

83. This passage is from Pietro Michiele's very loose translation in ottava rima of Ovid, *Ars amatoria* 1.507–509. See Ovid, *L'Arte degli amanti, di Pietro Michiele, nobile venetiano* (Venice: Giacomo Scaglia, 1632), 55 (canto 1, octave 67, lines 7–8).

84. Tarabotti ridicules the style of turned-up moustaches ("handlebar" moustaches) here, again later in this text, and especially in *Paternal Tyranny* (133) where she writes, in my translation: "How much more it is with envious spite than sincere truth that you call woman an imperfect animal, while you, who have hair on your face, and beastly behavior as well as unseemly visage, imitate brute animals,

A woman who has arrived at that age when her hair turns white proceeds to change its bright silver to gold, because she would not have her appearance seem less precious than her soul and wants all that is purest white to be enclosed in her heart and not shown on the outside. It is worse that men shave: they pluck and pull up by the roots the very virility of the hair on their chins that distinguishes them from a woman. Then when their hair begins to turn white, they let their beards grow, and now, at a time when they should begin to think about death, they begin to look like a man. Oh how he deceives himself, the foolish man who is rich in years and poor of wit!

And though he shaves and plucks	*E se ben rade e cava*
His old and prickling hairs,	*Il pel pungente e vecchio,*
Not for that his years are less, the days don't wash away,	*Però gli anni non scema, i dí non lava,*
Nor can his friendly mirror lie.	*Né bugie gli può dir l'amico specchio,*
Neither ambergris, nor scents most delicate	*Né l'ambra, né gli odor piú delicati*
Bring back the days gone by.	*Pon far tornar indietro i giorni andati.*[85]

If the vain adornments of women are dark shadows, as you say, it is there that men will find their rest, tranquility, and renewal. These are not men's shadows, since they are stable and not fleeting—and, because a shadow presupposes that there is light, nothing about wretched man can be called shadow since in him there is not even a scintilla, much less a ray of the light of any good quality at all.

You were right and perhaps prudent not to have considered the mirror and cosmetics while you enumerated every hair, indeed every minutia of women's extravagances and vanities. You have understood that your discourse can blush more without the one—that is, without painting its face—and without the other—that is, the mirror. A mirror should not be used by those who do not wish to recognize the defects of their own sex, nor to try to correct them in any way other than blaming unblemished women for what are indecorous excesses of male adornments.

---

and, in order to become in every way an unreasoning creature like those to whom nature gave horns, you have worked hard to succeed in raising those hairs on your face, precisely in the form of horns, anxious to imprint above your mouth, if not on your head, a sign that distinguishes you as a perfect animal."

85. These are lines sung by Aurora (soprano) in act 1, scene 7, of the dramma per musica *Gli amori d'Apollo e di Dafne* (libretto by Giovanni Francesco Busenello; music by Francesco Cavalli), first performed at carnival in Venice in 1640. See <http://www.librettidopera.it/apodafne/rid.html>. My thanks to Amyrose McCue Gill for this reference. Tarabotti was fond of Busenello's verse (see letters 104 and 112) and of him personally. In letter 152 she recounts the time he came masked to pay her a visit at Sant'Anna, full of compliments for her work.

Now, with your kind leave, Signor Buoninsegni, so that it be clear if you have rightly spoken or not, I wish to stage, before the eyes of the entire world, men dressed in the current fashion, and then you be the judge of whether your academic delirium—or let us say sick man's dream or yet a husband's lament—might have been put to better use in condemnation of men's rather than women's vanities. Imagine before your eyes these Polydoruses[86] who, after having worn out a half dozen combs on their long hair, as many warm irons on their beards, and a hundred other frivolities, leave the house to give the world a pompous vision of their good looks and affected dress. Just look at them, with their hair, not curly but curled, and with every strand so studiously placed that not even the brush of Apelles could do better.[87] Their beards and moustaches have been subjected in such a way to iron and fire that they have necessarily relinquished their natural form; both the former and the latter made so shiny by oil of jasmine, citron, or other, that they seem to be not hair but the finest silk. Is there anyone still who does not blush that his face reddens as he plucks and thins his eyebrows? But how could he blush? How could they fear shame who do not fear God?

Their dress is all lewdness, extravagance, and affectation. If it were not enough that they are made of silk plush, velvets, damasks. and other more sumptuous fabrics, they are also covered with lace. And they are fitted with a colored lining no less precious that shows in a thousand places, proving that if they dress in black they do so rather to conform to the style of the day and not because in their vain minds they do not prefer the frivolity of a thousand colors to the gravity of black. They also want it to be known that they wear a shirt of finest linen, so they let it show through in cuts made for that purpose and so that one can see that their shirt is embellished with Flemish embroidery and *punto in aria lace.*[88] They always have chains around their necks and bracelets on their wrists, a sign of their madness. Their collars and cuffs are worth a fortune, and to redouble the ostentation and expense they redouble the lists of lace and employ the finest cloth that Flanders can weave. Such grand champions as these always have with them an army of pendant cords ending in beads of silver and gold, ribbon bows, rings, laces, and a thousand various other eccentricities of so many colors that a peacock's tail

86. Polydoruses: favored sons. Polydoros in Homer, *Iliad* 20.407–410: "godlike Polydoros, / Priam's son, whom his father would not let go into battle / because he was youngest born of all his sons to him, and also / the most beloved." Homer, *Iliad*, trans. Richmond Lattimore (Chicago: University of Chicago Press, 1951). The name in Greek means "of many gifts."

87. Apelles of Kos, famous painter of ancient Greece (fl. 332–29 BCE). Tarabotti seems to refer here to Pliny the Elder's account of the fine lines of Apelles's brush strokes: *Historia naturalis* 35.81–82.

88. Raised needle lace. I quote the description by Lucrezia Marinella, *Essortazione* … (Venice: Valvasense, 1645), 97: "a type of handiwork called *punto in aria*, since it is made without being attached to cloth, in which you can see leaves, branches, flowers, and fruit." I have slightly adapted the translation in Lynn Lara Westwater, "The Disquieting Voice: Women's Writing and Antifeminism in Seventeenth-Century Venice" (PhD diss., University of Chicago, 2003), 1:141.

loses in comparison. On the other hand, precisely because they know they are just a lot of very vain peacocks, they do not want to be mortified, as the peacock is, by the sight of their deformed feet, so they cover them and dress them up at exorbitant expense.[89] They wear English hose on their legs, perhaps so their feet need not envy the insignia of the goddess Diana that many have on their heads, and many wear the form of the crescent moon also on the toe of their shoes, a veritable symbol of the fickleness of their brains.[90] And all the while, their unfortunate foot regrets it cannot show off its size, since, besides being pinched in and tormented by a tight shoe, it is surmounted by a rose so enormous that even if the foot were over two spans long it would look very small in comparison (fig. 10).[91]

We are down to the feet and so I was convinced I had finished describing the extravagances and vanities of men, but I have so much material that I do not want to neglect to mention some bagatelles that come to mind. I was right to call them bagatelles since they are indeed frivolities and childish things that make it very clear that, because they behave like children and become childlike, men dress like juveniles even in their old age. But let us forget about the frivolous things I alluded to—even though they suffice to show that their minds are immature—and consider some other aspects of their outward appearance.

Let those sashes they wrap around themselves tell you whether they have the minds of men or of children (even though they are richly embroidered, they are, nonetheless, swathes of cloth that prove they are like infants—not because of their innocence, but because of their vanity). Those suspenders (called *brazzaruola* in my city) that are attached to their shoulders to hold up their pants, are they not an invention that imitates the clothes of the tiniest toddlers? And that little bit of cloth, often covered with jewels and worn more for ostentation than to protect the stomach, is it not a very formal bib, like those worn by nursing babies? But if in their vanity they dress like the smallest babes, one would hope they would not incur gigantic expenses, or even that one might find a beautiful and precious body and soul beneath the beauty and richness of their garments and accoutrements.

Unfortunately, if their ornamented surface is sumptuous and attractive, their soul and body are filthy and deformed by a thousand sins and vices.

89. This comparison and reference to the peacock's embarrassment at the ugliness of its feet was perhaps suggested to Tarabotti by Valeriano's *Hieroglyphica*: "Il piú delle volte il fine delle ricchezze è brutto e dishonorato, & tali sono i piedi del pavone" (Most often the purpose of wealth is ugly and dishonorable, and so are the feet of the peacock). See Valeriano, *Ieroglifici*, 359. On the *Hieroglyphica*, see note 5 above.

90. The toe of English hose came to two points suggesting the shape of a crescent moon: Levi-Pisetzky, "Il gusto barocco," 79. The goddess Diana is represented with a crescent moon on her head. Tarabotti here alludes to the symbolic horns of men who are cuckolds. I have translated "leggera instabilità del loro cervello" as the "fickleness of their brains," hoping to capture the reference, clear in the word "instabilità," to the moon (and moon goddess Diana) as a symbol of inconstancy.

91. On their shoes men wore a large rose made of ribbon or a stiff knot that hung like moustaches, so large that they made it difficult to walk. See Levi-Pisetzky, "Il gusto barocco," 92.

Figure 10. Portrait of Lodovico Widmann (ca. 1637), by Tiberio Tinelli (1586–1638). National Gallery, Washington, D.C.

Are these not wasteful expenses and vanities, are they not, mister censor of feminine extravagances? Despite what you wish to think—pardon me if I speak too freely—they are wasteful expenses and vanities, so much more reprehensible in a man than in a woman, who was born to be the joy and splendor of humanity. In her, these things can be called rightfully and appropriately hers, but in him, who was born to embody fortitude and temperance, they are and always will be unfitting and indecent (figs. 10 and 11). Nevertheless, you do not mention men, while you speak ill of women. I well know why. It is because you are afraid of a bolt from the sky since you know how the gods have always championed the worth of women![92]

92. That the gods favor women is surely meant ironically, since Tarabotti has shown in an earlier passage that in myth the gods are cruel to women, they carry them off, or punish them unjustly for

Figure 11. The costume of a contemporary Venetian noble woman. Portrait of Signora Pantasilea Dotto Capodilista (ca. 1630), by Chiara Varotari (1584–1660/63). By kind permission of the Comune di Padova — Assessorato alla Cultura.

---

the transgressions of others. Understood in this way, the passage would mean that Buoninsegni could expect no retaliation from the gods for speaking against women, since both gods and men refuse to defend the worth of women. The irony, however, is not so obvious, since Tarabotti has shown earlier, with the example of Actaeon, that the gods punish men too for their offenses against women. In his *Censura* of the *Antisatira*, Ludovico Sesti takes the assertion literally and argues that the passage makes no sense because, knowing that the gods favor women, Buoninsegni should not have spoken against them: "*Unde hoc est?* Anzi sapendo questo dovea tacere"; Sesti, *Censura*, 174–75. He also suggests the possibility of a printer's error in the text. It seems to me to work as irony if we keep in mind that Tarabotti speaks against all who treat women badly, whether gods or men.

Oh, you would be a sorry one to preach for the good of souls, since you withhold out of fear what you should cry out to the stars! Indeed your kind of discourse makes me err: if until now I have spoken about men in general, I declare that I will, now and always, in this or any other writings of mine consider virtuous and good men who deserve it to be exceptions.

But how fortunate you are, Signor Buoninsegni, you who enjoy the protective shade and patronage of one of the most glorious princes who have ever lived in past centuries and who adorn the present.[93] Truly the influence of benevolent stars has favored your exceptional merit, allowing you to enjoy service to a prince, the brilliant splendors of whose blood, destined for the scepter of state, for power, and victories, are the least lights of his glory. Though it is true that he is not currently fighting on the fields of Mars, he would not, however, lack the spirit and strength to do so; and with his prayers turned to God he is taking part in those glorious victories that are supported by Tuscan forces in Italy under the leadership of the mighty arm of Prince Mattias.[94] This prince has to this day shown how one wins fighting—indeed, how one may, with his appearance alone, terrify and cut down enemies, conquer fortresses, and acquire the trophies of victory, and this is true now of the great Lorenzo's worthy heir in those heroic successes he is achieving in the service of his Catholic Majesty.

I imagine that the harsh criticism of women that Leopoldo has probably heard will have been ill received by that demigod whose every action is unblemished. I am certain that when necessary he would have his pen as well as his tongue ready to praise and protect that sex that deserves to be defended by every hero's voice and compositions. Clearly he shows himself to be our tutelary deity, since in his qualities and manners the goddesses are sculpted: in his looks we find Celestial Venus, in his intellect Pallas Athena, Diana in his chastity, Minerva in his wisdom, the Graces in his movements and gentility, and he is that Apollo adored by all the Muses. To confound the vanity of other men he does not appear adorned in garments more sumptuous and expensive than a clerical toga, perhaps because it is dress not far different from that of women.[95] When that most happy day will come that he will do honor to a purple Vatican hat, and from that

93. Leopoldo de' Medici. See note 17 above.

94. Prince Mattias de' Medici (1613–1667), brother of Leopoldo, Giancarlo, and the Grand Duke Ferdinando II, was governor of Siena and commander of the Tuscan military forces. In 1632, Mattias was sent to Germany to learn the military art in the service of the Holy Roman Emperor Ferdinand II. He fought in Austria with the Hapsburgs during the Thirty Years War and, returning to Tuscany in 1641, he was commander of the Tuscan army in the War of Castro and then of the league of Venice, Parma, Mantua, and Tuscany.

95. Leopoldo de' Medici was made cardinal only in 1667, but as a young man he had his portrait painted in clerical dress, which was not unusual for the time, and in several portraits as an adult he is seen in black with white collar and cuffs. See Karla Langedijk, *The Portraits of the Medici, Fifteenth to Eighteenth Centuries* (Florence: Studio per Edizioni Scelte, 1981–1983), 2:1104–1120.

purple ascend to the throne of Peter, then the most peaceful time of the sacrosanct Medici lions will return.[96] No longer will poor Italy see her veins opened up by the swords of her sons and drown in her own blood, but the Christian world will rest in the shade of olive trees cultivated and nurtured by the great shepherd Leopoldo, for the quiet and protection of the dear flocks given to his keeping by the divine hand of God.[97] For now he loves to have his hair cut short and adorned by a cleric's cap, unlike vain, mad men, whose curls toss in the wind, and it shall be that, instead of other jewels, he will bejewel his garments with the precious rubies of the blood of Christ.[98]

If all men were like him, my pen would not reproach them for their vanities, nor would we read satires that censure, but rather panegyrics that exalt those of women, which are as appropriate and necessary as are the embellishments of sacred objects, and as women and their beauty are necessary for the preservation of humankind.

Were you to imitate your patron, you would not have to fear meeting with an unhappy fate such as that of Orpheus. But I take this to be more a fervent desire of yours than a fear, since, as they say, you run two errands on a single excursion:[99] you make women seem to be more cruel than the Furies of Hell and you compare yourself to Orpheus. Were he alive today, men would scarcely be worthy of joining the other unreasoning beings to follow along and to listen to him.[100] What is said of the Maenads is untrue, and yet the abuses of those times permitted—indeed honored—furious and mad excesses such as the sacrifices made to Bacchus. It could be that the women of Thrace were shown to be pious rather than evil and cruel when they conferred a merited death on that profane singer, to whom you, sir, are alike, no less for the sweetness of your song than for your abhorrence of women. But the pages of ancient and modern times are filled with a thousand tragic stories that show wicked man to be the most cruel and fierce animal alive. Unfortunately, Neros and Maxentiuses are with us even in present times.[101] How

96. By Tarabotti's time there had been three Medici popes, of whom two had taken the name Leo, Leone (meaning lion) in Italian: Giovanni de' Medici, Leo X (1513–1521); Giulio de' Medici, Clement VII (1523–1534); and Alessandro de' Medici, Leo XI (April 1–27, 1605).

97. Tarabotti seems to believe that as early as the 1640s, Leopoldo was being considered for a cardinal's hat. His brother Giancarlo was made cardinal in 1644.

98. The color of a cardinal's robe.

99. Tarabotti uses the idiomatic expression "fate … in un viaggio due servigi," which I have chosen to translate literally: to run two errands (services) on a single excursion. The English expression to kill two birds with one stone is close in meaning, but I think the hunting context to which it belongs would be incongruous in Tarabotti's lexicon.

100. Tarabotti puts men in the same category of unreasoning beings as the trees, stones, and wild animals that were attracted by the music of Orpheus.

101. Nero Claudius Caesar (37–68 CE) and Marcus Aurelius Valerius Maxentius (278–312 CE), Roman emperors known for their cruelty.

many, oh how many examples there are today of cruelty, injustice, and evil! One brother kills the other for no reason except the fear of losing his inheritance. Men kill women to obtain a bit of gold, acts no less wicked than those of ancients like Anaxarchus, who was pounded to death in a mortar, and Perillus, the inventor of machines of torture.[102]

You would do well to find another shelter from the fulminations of women than laurel trees. Daphne would feel obliged rather to hit you across the shoulders with her trunk than to adorn your temples with her leaves. And you, chivalrous gentleman that you are, must enjoy such blows more than the most sublime honors that Apollo bestows on you, since you are clearly offering her the occasion.

One who has committed a serious crime must seek to provide himself with adequate protection. Having offended women, the most beautiful and worthy creatures to come from the hands of God, you implore the protection of the most glorious and worthy prince that God has destined for crown and scepter.[103] His protection, if you obtain it, could not be more secure and auspicious for you, since he could defend you from the thunderbolts of Jove not merely those of women; but I fear the contrary, because the great Ferdinando, accustomed and dedicated to defending virtue, will not wish to share the aura of his generous patronage with a pen and tongue that find ways to devote themselves to disparaging that sex which, by producing subjects for them, princes can only love and esteem.

I, instead, and not in vain, will implore his justice and, emboldened, I will denounce you before the tribunal of his scorn because, having dared to disparage the worth of women without making even one exception, you have become guilty of *lèse majesté* against his Most Serene wife.[104] She alone should suffice to make even the most daring wit refuse to disparage women, since in her alone are qualities sufficient to bestow glory on the entire sex. Even though princesses of her rank, demigoddesses that they are, must be separated out from the multitude of other women, this is accidental and related to their worth and not substantial

102. Anaxarchus of Abdera (fourth century BCE), a Greek philosopher pounded to death in a mortar by Nicocreon, King of Cyprus, for having, it seems, expressed the wish for the king's decapitation. See Diogenes Laertius, *Lives of Eminent Philosophers*, trans. R. D. Hicks (Cambridge, MA: Harvard University Press, 1995), 470–73 (9.10). The Greek architect Perillus built an instrument of torture for Phalaris, tyrant of Agrigento, a hollow bronze bull in which to roast his enemies; he became Phalaris's first victim. Many sources were available to Tarabotti: Dante, for example, refers to this story in *Inferno* 27.7. The examples of both Anaxarchus and Perillus are recounted in Tommaso Garzoni, *Il teatro dei vari e diversi cervelli mondani*, ed. Paolo Cherchi (Ravenna: Longo Editore, 1993), 204, 231 (discourses 30, 47). With these two examples of men who wished ill on others and who became victims themselves, Tarabotti seems to suggest that men who treat women badly may expect to be punished for it. Perhaps it is a reference to her verbal punishment of men in the *Antisatira*.

103. Buoninsegni dedicates his satire to Grand Duke Ferdinando II de' Medici, who was in attendance at the academy meeting when Buoninsegni delivered his discourse.

104. Vittoria della Rovere, to whom Tarabotti dedicates her *Antisatira*.

and related to their nature. And it is indeed because of her goodness that the Most Serene Grand Duchess has taken up the arms of holy prayers and spiritual exercises (since in turbulent times such as these in Italy she is not allowed to carry a sword and shield into battle), and this is perhaps why phalanxes and armies of angels have come to protect the Tuscan forces.

But perhaps I have dared too much by trying with my lowly pen to fly to such lofty places as those Highnesses, which one should revere rather than praise. I will say no more, Signor Buoninsegni. I leave you with your conscience to reprimand you gravely for having offended the truth, and with the understanding that women, who are innocent, good, and aware of their own worth, hold in no account the lying conceits of those who cannot with the blackness of their inks tarnish the purest candor of the most glorious merits of which women are so proud, since

A cloud, that with the favor of fierce winds	*Nube, che col favor di fieri venti,*
Veils the sun and drains the world of color,	*Al sol fa velo e 'l mondo discolora,*
Takes not away the sun's resplendent rays;	*Non toglie al sole i raggi suoi lucenti;*
Nor does its power wane if at times	*Né perde il pregio suo benché talora*
A resounding cittern plucked by a rude hand	*Noiosi esprima e mal temprati accenti*
Sounds tedious and ill-tempered notes.	*Tocca da rozza man cetra canora.*[105]

105. I have not been able to identify the author of these lines. Perhaps they are Tarabotti's own.

Bibliography

Works by Buoninsegni and Tarabotti

Buoninsegni, Francesco. *Il lusso donnesco, Satira menippea.* Milan: Filippo Ghisolfi, 1637.

———. *Del lusso donnesco, Satira menippea ... con l'Antisatira apologetica di Giovanni Battista Torretti,* 1–44. Venice: Giacomo Sarzina, 1638.

———. *Contro 'l lusso donnesco, Satira menippea del Sig. Fran. Buoninsegni con l'Antisatira [di] D[onna] A[rcangela] T[arabotti] in risposta,* 19–63. Venice: Francesco Valvasense, 1644 V1.

———. *Contro 'l lusso donnesco, Satira menippea del Sig. Fran. Buoninsegni con l'Antisatira [di] D[onna] A[rcangela] T[arabotti] in risposta,* 19–65. Venice: Francesco Valvasense, 1644 V2.

———. *Contro 'l lusso donnesco* [1656]. In Sesti, *Censura,* 7–28.

———. *Satira.* In Buoninsegni and Tarabotti, *Satira e Antisatira,* 38–55.

———. *Delle sciocchezze degli huomini,* 1650. Florence, Biblioteca Nazionale Centrale (BNCF), Magliabechi VII 456, fols. 53r–84r (fair copy); fols. 97r–109v (incomplete autograph copy).

Buoninsegni, Francesco, and Arcangela Tarabotti. *Satira e Antisatira.* Edited by Elissa Weaver. Rome: Salerno Editrice, 1998.

Sesti, Ludovico. *Censura dell'Antisatira della signora Angelica* [sic] *Tarabotti fatta in risposta alla Satira menippea, Contro il lusso donnesco del sig. Franc. Buoninsegni scherzo geniale di Lucido Ossiteo* [pseud.] *accadem. aristocratico.* Siena: Bonetti, 1656.

Tarabotti, Arcangela. *Antisatira.* In Buoninsegni, *Contro 'l lusso donnesco* (1644, V1), 3–13, 72–227.

———. *Antisatira.* In Buoninsegni, *Contro 'l lusso donnesco* (1644, V2), 3–13, 67–229.

———. *Antisatira.* In Sesti, *Censura,* 29–104.

———. *Antisatira.* In Buoninsegni and Tarabotti, *Satira e Antisatira,* 31–33, 36–105.

———. *Che le donne siano della spetie degli huomini: Difesa della donna di Galerana Barcitotti* [pseud.] *contra Horatio Plata il traduttore di quei fogli che dicono le donne non essere della spetie degli huomini.* Nuremberg: Iuvan Cherchenbergher [fictitious place and publisher], 1651.

———. *Che le donne siano della spezie degli uomini: Women Are No Less Rational Than Men.* Edited by Letizia Panizza. London: Institute of Romance Studies, 1994.

———. *Convent Paradise.* Edited and translated by Meredith K. Ray and Lynn Lara Westwater. Toronto: Iter Press; Tempe, AZ: Arizona Center for Medieval and Renaissance Studies, 2020.

———. *L'"Inferno monacale" di Arcangela Tarabotti.* Edited by Francesca Medioli. Turin: Rosenberg & Sellier, 1990.

———. *Lettere familiari e di complimento* and *Le Lagrime d'Arcangela Tarabotti per la morte dell'illustrissima Signora Regina Donati.* Venice: Guerigli, 1650.

———. *Lettere familiari e di complimento.* Edited by Meredith Ray and Lynn Westwater. Turin: Rosenberg & Sellier, 2005.

———. *Letters Familiar and Formal.* Edited and translated by Meredith K. Ray and Lynn Lara Westwater. Toronto: Iter, Inc. and Centre for Reformation and Renaissance Studies, 2012.

———. *Il Paradiso monacale, libri tre, con un soliloquio a Dio.* Venice: Guglielmo Oddoni, 1643.

———. *Paternal Tyranny.* Edited and translated by Letizia Panizza. Chicago: University of Chicago Press, 2004.

———. *La Semplicità ingannata di Galerana Baratotti* [pseud.]. Leiden: Gio. Sambix [Daniel and Jean Elzevir], 1654. [304 pp.]

———. *La Semplicità ingannata di Galerana Baratotti* [pseud.]. Leiden: Gio. Sambix [fictitious place, probably Venice], 1654. [191 pp.] Pirate edition.

———. *La semplicità ingannata: Edizione critica e commentata.* Edited by Simona Bortot. Padua: Il Poligrafo, 2007.

———. *Women Are of the Human Species.* In Kenney, *"Women Are Not Human,"* 87–159. Translation of *Che le donne siano della spetie degli huomini.*

Other Primary Sources

Acidalius, Valens [Valtin Havekenthal; attributed]. *Disputatio nova contra mulieres, qua probatur eas homines non esse.* [Zerbst, Germany]: n.p., 1595. Critical bilingual edition by Clive Hart: *Disputatio nova contra mulieres: A New Argument against Women: A Critical Translation from the Latin with Commentary, Together with the Original Latin Text of 1595* (Lewiston, NY: Edwin Mellen Press, 1998).

Anonymous. *Che le donne non siano della spetie degli huomini: Discorso piacevole tradotto da Oratio Plata romano.* Lyon: Per Gasparo Ventura [but Venice: Francesco Valvasense], 1647.

———. *Le glorie degli Incogniti, overo Gli hvomini illvstri dell'Accademia de' Signori Incogniti di Venetia.* Venice: Valvasense, 1647.

Aprosio, Angelico. *La biblioteca aprosiana, passatempo autunnale di Cornelio Apasio Antivigilmi* [pseud.]. Bologna: Per li Manolessi, 1673.

———. *"La Maschera scoperta" di Filofilo Misoponero* [pseud.] *in risposta all' "Antisatira" di D. A. T. scritta contro la "Satira menippea" del signor Francesco Buoninsegni.* In Biga, *Una polemica antifemminista*, 93–174.

———. *Lo Scudo di Rinaldo, overo Lo specchio del disinganno, opera di Scipio Glareano* [pseud.] Venice: Gio. Iacomo Hertz, 1646.

Arnigio, Bartolomeo. *Le dieci veglie di B. Arnigio degli ammendati costumi dell' humana vita.* Brescia: Francesco e Pietro Maria fratelli de' Marchetti, 1577.

Ariosto, Ludovico. *Orlando furioso (The Frenzy of Orlando): A Romantic Epic.* Translated by Barbara Reynolds. 2 vols. London: Penguin, 1975, 1977.

———. *Orlando furioso.* Edited by Cesare Segre. 5th ed. Milan: Mondadori, 1990.

Bissari, Pietro Paolo. *Le scorse olimpiche, trattenimenti accademici.* Venice: Francesco Valvasense, 1648.

Busenello, Giovanni Francesco, librettist. *Gli amori d'Apollo e di Dafne.* Music by Francesco Cavalli. Venice, 1640. <http://www.librettidopera.it/apodafne/rid.html>.

Capra, Galeazzo Flavio. *Della eccellenza e dignità delle donne.* Edited by Maria Luisa Doglio. Rome: Bulzoni Editori, 1988. First printed 1525.

Cartari, Vincenzo. *Le immagini de i dei degli antichi.* Edited by Ginetta Auzzas, Federica Martignago, Manlio Pastore Stocchi, and Paola Rigo. Vicenza: Neri Pozza, 1996. First printed 1556.

Erasmus. *Opera omnia.* Edited by Jean Le Clerc. 10 vols. Leiden: Petrus Vander, 1703–1706.

Fonte, Moderata [pseud. of Modesta Pozzo]. *Il merito delle donne ... ove chiaramente si scuopre quanto siano elle degne e piú perfette de gli huomini.* Venice: Domenico Imberti, 1600.

Garzoni, Tomaso. *Il teatro dei vari e diversi cervelli mondani.* In Tomaso Garzoni, *Opere*, edited by Paolo Cherchi (Ravenna: Longo, 1993).

Genuzio, Andrea. *Satira ed Antisatira.* Edited by Girolamo De Miranda. Rome: Salerno Editrice, 1997. First printed 1640 with title *Satira ed Antisatira contro gli abbigliamenti degli uomini e delle donne.*

Ghilini, Girolamo. *Teatro d'huomini letterati.* Venice: Guerigli, 1647.

Guarini, Battista. *Il pastor fido.* Edited by Elisabetta Selmi. Venice: Marsilio, 1999.

———. *Il pastor fido: The Faithfull Shepherd.* Edited by J. H. Whitfield. Translated by Richard Fanshawe (1647). Austin: University of Texas Press, 1976.

Hesiod. *Theogony.* Translated by Hugh G. Evelyn-White. Internet Sacred Text Archive, 1914. <http://www.sacred-texts.com/cla/hesiod/theogony.htm>.

Homer. *Iliad.* Translated by Richmond Lattimore. Chicago: University of Chicago Press, 1951.

Kenney, Theresa M., ed. and trans. "*Women are Not Human*": *An Anonymous Treatise and Responses.* New York: Crossroad Publishing, 1998.

Laertius, Diogenes. *Lives of Eminent Philosophers.* Translated by R. D. Hicks. 2 vols. Cambridge, MA: Harvard University Press, 1995. Orig. 1925.

Lampugnani, Agostino. *Carrozza da nolo, overo Del vestire e usanze alla moda, di Gio. Sonta Pagnalmino* [pseud.] Bologna: Carlo Zenero, 1648. Reprinted: Milan: Lodovico Monza, 1649; Venice: Giacomo Bortoli, 1655.

Loredano, Giovanni Francesco. *Lettere del Signor Gio. Francesco Loredano, nobile veneto, divise in cinquantadue capi, e raccolte da Henrico Giblet* [pseud.]. Venice: Guerigli, 1657.

Macrobius. *Saturnalia*. Translated by Robert A. Kaster. Vol. 1. Cambridge, MA: Harvard University Press, 2011.

Marinella, Lucrezia. *Essortazione* .... Venice: Valvasense, 1645.

Martial. *M. Valerii Martialis Epigrammaton libri*. Edited by Ludwig Friedlaender. 2 vols. Leipzig: S. Hirzel, 1886.

Opere di Gabriello Chiabrera e Fulvio Testi. Milan: Nicolò Bettoni, 1834.

Orsini, Cesare. *Diporti poetici*. Venice: Evangelista Deuchino, 1630.

Ovid. *The Art of Love and Other Poems*. Translated by J. H. Mozley. 2nd ed., revised by G. P. Goold. Cambridge, MA: Harvard University Press; London: William Heinemann, 1979.

———. *L'arte degli amanti, di Pietro Michiele, nobile venetiano*. Venice: Giacomo Scaglia, 1632. Translation of Ovid, *Ars amatoria*.

———. *Le metamorfosi d'Ovidio, ridatte da Giovanni Andrea dell'Anguillara in ottava rima*. Milan: Dalla Società tipografica de' classici italiani, 1805.

Pers, Ciro di. *Poesie*. Edited by Michele Rak. Turin: Einaudi, 1978.

Petrarca, Francesco. *Canzoniere*. Edited by Marco Santagata. Milan: Mondadori, 1996.

———. *Canzoniere*. Translated by J. G. Nichols. New York: Routledge, 2002. Orig. Manchester: Carcanet, 2000.

———. *The Triumphs of Love: Chastitie: Death*. Translated by Anna Hume. Edinburgh: Evan Tyler, 1644.

———. *The Triumphs of Petrarch*. Translated by Ernest Hatch Wilkins. Chicago: University of Chicago Press, 1962.

———. *Triumphus cupidinis*. Edited by Vinicio Pacca. In Francesco Petrarca, *Trionfi, Rime estravaganti, Codice degli abbozzi*, edited by Vinicio Pacca and Laura Paolino, 47–220. Milan: Mondadori, 1996.

Ramusio, Giovanni Battista. *Navigazioni e viaggi*. Edited by Marica Milanesi. 6 vols. Turin: Einaudi, 1978–1988.

Ravisius Textor, Johannes (Jean Tixier de Ravisi). *Officina, sive theatrum historicum et poeticum* .... Basel: Sumptibus Ludovici Regis, 1617.

Recueil général de coeffures de différents gouts, ou l'on voit la manière dont se coëffoient les femmes, sous différents règnes, à commencer en 1589 jusqu'en 1778. Paris: Desnos, 1778.

Ricchieri, Lodovico [Celio Rhodigino]. *Lodovici Caelii Rhodigini Lectionvm antiqvarum libri XXX*, Book 15, Chapter 8: *Charilaum interogatum cur coman nutriret, respondisse, Quoniam ex omni ornatu hic pulchrior foret, venustiorque, ac sumpus minimi*. Lyon: apud Sebastianum Honoratum, 1560.

Tasso, Torquato. *Gerusalemme liberata*. Edited by Lanfranco Caretti. Turin: Einaudi, 1971. Reprint 1993.

———. *The Liberation of Jerusalem*. Translated by Max Wickert. Oxford: Oxford University Press, 2009.

Torretti, Giovanni Battista. *Per il lusso donnesco antisatira apologetica*. Venice: G. Sarzina, 1638.

Valeriano, Pierio. *Ieroglifici, overo Commentari delle occulte significationi de gli Egittij, & d'altre nationi*. Venice: Gio. Antonio and Giacomo Franceschi, 1602.

Secondary Sources

Ago, Renata. *Il gusto delle cose: Una storia degli oggetti nella Roma del Seicento.* Rome: Donzelli, 2006.

Asor-Rosa, Alberto. "Aprosio, Angelico, detto il Ventimiglia." In *Dizionario biografico degli italiani*, 3 (1961): 650–53. <http://www.treccani.it/enciclopedia/aprosio-angelico-detto-il-ventimiglia_%28Dizionario-Biografico%29/>.

Baldini, Massimo, Marica Spalletti, and Maria Vittoria Adelman, eds. *La moda capelli: La storia, le teorie, e i dati di tipo visuale*. Rome: Armando, 2006.

Benadusi, Giovanna. "Carteggi e negozi della granduchessa Vittoria della Rovere, 1634–1694." In *Le donne Medici nel sistema europeo delle corti, XVI–XVIII secolo: Atti del convegno internazionale, Firenze, San Domenico di Fiesole, 6–8 ottobre 2005*, edited by Giulia Calvi and Riccardo Spinelli, 1:415–31. Florence: Polistampa, 2008.

———. "The Gender Politics of Vittoria della Rovere." In *Medici Women: The Making of a Dynasty in Grand Ducal Tuscany*, edited by Giovanna Benadusi and Judith C. Brown, 265–301. Toronto: Centre for Reformation and Renaissance Studies, 2015.

Biga, Emilia, ed. *Una polemica antifemminista del '600: "La maschera scoperta" di Anglico Aprosio.* Ventimiglia: Civica Biblioteca Aprosiana, 1989.

Bortot, Simona. "Introduzione: La penna all'ombra delle grate." In Tarabotti, *La semplicità ingannata,* ed. Bortot, 21–152.

Bufacchi, Emanuela. "'La mia semplicità è stata ingannata dalla sagacia del serpente': Polemiche di Girolamo Brusoni con Arcangela Tarabotti." *Esperienze letterarie* 40, no. 2 (2015): 55–77.

Canepa, Nancy L. "The Writing Behind the Wall: Arcangela Tarabotti's 'Inferno monacale' and Cloistral Autobiography in the Seventeenth Century." *Forum italicum* 30, no. 1 (1996): 1–23.

Capucci, Martino. "Francesco Buoninsegni." In *Dizionario biografico degli italiani,* 15 (1972): 254–55. <http://www.treccani.it/enciclopedia/francesco-buoninsegni_%28Dizionario-Biografico%29/>

Cipolla, Carlo M. *Fighting the Plague in Seventeenth-Century Italy*. Madison: University of Wisconsin Press, 1981.

Conti Odorisio, Ginevra. *Donne e società nel Seicento: Lucrezia Marinelli e Arcangela Tarabotti.* Rome: Bulzoni, 1979.

———. *Storia dell'idea femminista in Italia.* Turin: ERI, 1980.

Costa-Zalessow, Natalia. "La condanna all''Indice' della 'Semplicità ingannata' di Arcangela Tarabotti alla luce di manoscritti inediti." *Nouvelles de la république des lettres* 1 (2002): 97–113.

———. "Tarabotti's 'La semplicità ingannata' and Its Twentieth-Century Interpreters, with Unpublished Documents Regarding Its Condemnation to the 'Index.'" *Italica* 78 (2001): 314–25.

De Caro, Gaspare. "Girolamo Brusoni." In *Dizionario biografico degli italiani,* 14 (1972): 712–20. <http://www.treccani.it/enciclopedia/girolamo-brusoni_%28Dizionario-Biografico%29/>.

Dizionario biografico degli italiani. Rome: Istituto dell'Enciclopedia Italiana, 1960– . <http://www.treccani.it/biografie/>.

Infelise, Mario. "Books and Politics in Arcangela Tarabotti's Venice." In Weaver, *Arcangela Tarabotti,* 57–72.

———. "Ex ignotus notus? Note sul tipografo Sarzina e l'Accademia degli Incogniti." In *Libri, tipografi, biblioteche: Ricerche storiche dedicate a Luigi Balsamo,* edited by Arnaldo Ganda, 207–23. Florence: Olschki, 1997.

———. "Libri e politica nella Venezia di Arcangela Tarabotti." *Annali di storia moderna e contemporanea* 8 (2002): 32–45.

Kelly, Joan. "Early Feminist Theory and the *Querelle des Femmes.*" In *Women, History, and Theory: The Essays of Joan Kelly,* 65–109. Chicago: University of Chicago Press, 1984.

Kirk, Eugene P. *Menippean Satire: An Annotated Catalogue of Texts and Criticism.* New York: Garland Publishing, 1980.

Langedijk, Karla. *The Portraits of the Medici, Fifteenth to Eighteenth Centuries.* Vol. 2. Florence: Studio per Edizioni Scelte, 1981–1983.

Levi-Pisetzky, Rita. *Il costume e la moda nella società italiana.* Turin: Einaudi, 1978.

———. "Il gusto barocco nel costume italiano del Seicento." *Studi secenteschi* 2 (1961): 61–94.

———. *Storia del costume in Italia.* Vol. 3: *Il Seicento.* Rome: Istituto Editoriale Italiano, 1966.

Lissoni, Nicoletta. "La 'ragion di stato' monacale nel pensiero di Arcangela Tarabotti." In *Amazzoni, sante, ninfe: Variazioni di storia delle idee dall'antichità al Rinascimento,* edited by Davide Bigalli, 247–60. Milan: Cortina, 2006.

Magnanini, Suzanne, and David Lamari. "Giuseppe Passi's Attacks on Women in 'The Defects of Women.'" In *In Dialogue with the Other Voice in Sixteenth-Century Italy: Literary and Social Contexts for Women's Writing,* edited by Julie D. Campbell and Maria Galli Stampino, 143–94. Toronto: Iter Inc. and Centre for Reformation and Renaissance Studies, 2011.

Marini, Quinto. "Angelico Aprosio da Ventimiglia 'tromba per far conoscer molti.'" In Quinto Marini, *Frati barocchi: Studi su A. G. Brignole Sale, G. A. De Marini, A. Aprosio, F. F. Frugoni, P. Segneri*, 153–79. Modena: Mucchi, 2000.

Mazzuchelli, Giammaria. *Gli scrittori d'Italia, cioè Notizie storiche e critiche intorno alle vite e agli scritti dei letterati italiani*. Vol. 2. Brescia: Giambattista Bossini, 1763.

Medioli, Francesca. "Arcangela Tarabotti's Reliability about Herself: Publication and Self-Representation (Together with a Small Collection of Previously Unpublished Letters)." *The Italianist* 23 (2003): 54–101.

———. "Alcune lettere autografe di Arcangela Tarabotti: Autocensura e immagine di sé." *Rivista di storia e letteratura religiosa* 32 (1996): 133–55.

———. "Des liaisons dangereuses? Réseaux hérités, supposés, et déguisés d'une nonne vénitienne au XVIIe siècle." *Genre & histoire* 11 (Fall 2012). <http://journals.openedition.org/genrehistoire/1750>.

———. "Monacazioni forzate: Donne ribelli al proprio destino." *Clio: Trimestrale di studi storici* 30 (1994): 431–54.

Melchor i Fenollosa, Roser. "Sonets esparsos de Francesco Buoninsegni." PhD diss., University of Valencia, 2005.

Panizza, Letizia. "Volume Editor's Introduction." In Tarabotti, *Paternal Tyranny*, 1–31.

Paulicelli, Eugenia. "*La moda* and Its Technologies: Agostino Lampugnani's 'La carrozza da nolo, ovvero del vestire e usanze alla moda': The Rented Carriage, or Of Clothing and Fashionable Habits, 1648–1650." In Paulicelli, *Writing Fashion*, 205–23.

———. "Sister Arcangela Tarabotti: Hair, Wigs and Other Vices." In Paulicelli, *Writing Fashion*, 177–204.

———. *Writing Fashion in Early Modern Italy: From "Sprezzatura" to Satire*. Aldershot, Farnham, Surrey, UK: Ashgate, 2014.

Pignatti, Franco. "Cesare Orsini." In *Dizionario biografico degli italiani*, 79 (2013): 629–32. <http://www.treccani.it/enciclopedia/cesare-orsini_%28Dizionario-Biografico%29/ >.

Portigliotti, Giuseppe. *Penombre claustrali*. Milan: Fratelli Treves, 1930.

Ray, Meredith K. "Letters and Lace: Arcangela Tarabotti and Convent Culture in Seicento Venice." In *Early Modern Women and Transnational Communities of Letters*, edited by Julie Campbell and Ann Larsen, 45–73. Aldershot, Farnham, Surrey, UK: Ashgate, 2009.

Schutte, Anne Jacobson. *By Force and Fear: Taking and Breaking Monastic Vows in Early Modern Europe*. Ithaca, NY: Cornell University Press, 2011.

Sperling, Jutta G. *Convents and the Body Politic in Late Renaissance Venice*. Chicago: University of Chicago Press, 1999.

Spini, Giorgio. *Ricerca dei libertini: La teoria dell'impostura delle religioni nel Seicento italiano*. Florence: La Nuova Italia, 1983.

Straussman-Pflanzer, Eve. "Court Culture in Seventeenth-Century Florence: The Art Patronage of Medici Grand Duchess Vittoria della Rovere (1622–1694)." PhD diss., New York University Institute of Fine Arts, 2010.

Valenti, Margherita. "Sant'Anna di Castello: Inventario archivistico di un monastero benedettino femminile." PhD diss., University of Ca' Foscari, Venice, 2005–2006.

Weaver, Elissa B., ed. *Arcangela Tarabotti: A Literary Nun in Baroque Venice.* Ravenna: Longo, 2006.

———. "'With Truthful Tongue and Faithful Pen': Arcangela Tarabotti against Paternal Tyranny." In *Speaking Truth to Power from Medieval to Modern Italy,* edited by Jo Ann Cavallo and Carlo Lottieri, 281–96. *Annali d'italianistica* 34 (2016).

Westwater, Lynn Lara. "The Disquieting Voice: Women's Writing and Antifeminism in Seventeenth-Century Venice." PhD diss., University of Chicago, 2003.

———. "A Rediscovered Friendship in the Republic of Letters: The Unpublished Correspondence of Arcangela Tarabotti and Ismaël Boulliau." *Renaissance Quarterly* 65, no. 1 (2012): 67–134.

Zanette, Emilio. *Suor Arcangela: Monaca del Seicento veneziano.* Venice: Istituto per la collaborazione culturale, 1960.

Zarri, Gabriella. "Monasteri femminili e città, secoli XV–XVIII." In *Storia d'Italia: Annali,* vol. 9: *La Chiesa e il potere politico dal Medioevo all'età contemporanea,* edited by Giorgio Chittolini and Giovanni Miccoli, 357–429. Turin: Einaudi, 1986.

———. "Monasteri femminili in Italia nel secolo XVI." In Gabriella Zarri, Francesca Medioli, and Paola Vismara Chiappa, "'De Monialibus,' secoli XVI–XVII–XVIII." *Rivista di storia e letteratura religiosa* 33 (1997): 643–69.

Index

Page numbers that refer to illustrations are in italics.